ADVANCE PRAISE FOR *SHARED IMAGINATION*

Shared Imagination by Mary Ann Archer is an intimately graceful and thoughtful work of spirituality, a book teeming with Spirit. And it is a daring book—because it presumes God has more for us all the time, and because it shows us ways to access and share that more.

The heart of this book lies in the myriad experiences of actual spiritual aliveness occurring in the lives of women, and some men, who participate in group (and individual) spiritual direction. The specificity, the color, the ah-hah moments, the depth of self-realization, the awareness of God on the move in each life is breathtaking.

Rev. Dr. Robin Hawley Gorsline, (he,him; they,them) Poet*Queer Theologian

MARY ANN ARCHER CAN ENHANCE YOUR RELATIONSHIP WITH GOD - AND OTHERS WHO LOVE HIM!

Margaret Bigger, author of 14 non-fiction books

Shared Imagination offers us a groundbreaking application of Ignatian imaginative prayer practices to group spiritual direction. Firmly rooted in scriptural and spiritual tradition, each group meeting using this approach includes imaginative meditation, confidential conversation, and a closing worship service.

This rich resource is highly recommended for use by spiritual directors and others interested in spiritual growth group work. It offers not only a sound introduction but also vivid glimpses into what people have experienced in these groups.

Dr. Anne Winchell Silver, Director of Spiritual Direction Programs, The General Theological Seminary, NY, NY; author, *Trustworthy Connections: Interpersonal Issues in Spiritual Direction*

SHARED IMAGINATION

A Channel to God and with Each Other

MARY ANN ARCHER

BALBOA.
PRESS

A DIVISION OF HAY HOUSE

Balboa Press books may be ordered through booksellers or by contacting:

Balboa Press
A Division of Hay House
1663 Liberty Drive
Bloomington, IN 47403
www.balboapress.com
1 (877) 407-4847

Scripture quotations are from New Revised Standard Version Bible, copyright © 1989 National Council of the Churches of Christ in the United States of America. Used by permission. All rights reserved.

Other Notes:
The New Oxford Annotated Bible, New Revised Standard Version, passages
The Book of Common Worship, 9 prayers
The Episcopal Book of Common Prayer, 8 passages in the service of Compline.
The New Zealand Episcopal Book of Common Prayer, a version of the Lord's Prayer.

Print information available on the last page.

ISBN: 978-1-9822-0372-6 (sc)
ISBN: 978-1-9822-0374-0 (hc)
ISBN: 978-1-9822-0373-3 (e)

Library of Congress Control Number: 2018905405

Balboa Press rev. date: 10/02/2018

To Pamela Barnett—soul friend, mentor, shepherdess—who opened the door.

CONTENTS

FOREWORD

Shared Imagination by Mary Ann Archer is an intimately graceful and thoughtful work of spirituality, a book teeming with Spirit. And it is a daring book—because it presumes God has more for us all the time and because it shows us ways to access and share that more.

Unlike traditional biblical study, with emphasis on what the text means or making a point about an issue or concern, Archer uses biblical texts and other resources to help participants in her spiritual direction groups begin to experience the story/text in their own ways and lives— to let the stories and the imaginings arising in response take them to new places or visit ones long forgotten.

The heart of this book lies in the myriad experiences of actual spiritual aliveness occurring in the lives of women, and some men, who participate in group (and individual) spiritual direction. The specificity, the color, the ah-ha moments, the depth of self-realization, the awareness of God on the move in each life is breathtaking. As Archer records her own awareness of the power she feels in participation in the weekly groups, led by her mentor who began the process in their local church—"It was," she says, "my native land"—so too do so many others convey the same deep spiritual awareness. One can see these pilgrims taking root in gentle, safe, inviting soil and blooming with new and growing spiritual health.

The use of all five senses is essential to the process. No thought, no imagining, is too wild. Jesus shows up in all sorts of ways, even in costumes a long way removed from ancient Palestine. Nor are biblical passages the only place to start. One of the most intriguing meditations focuses on the meditator entering a room in which a nude statue is at the center. After examining the statue, the person becomes the statue;

then Jesus enters the room and speaks to the person/statue. The goal is for the subject to feel whatever comes and to see what deep personal truth(s) may emerge.

Another involved a man in individual spiritual direction by phone being open to an email, with attachments, from God. The imaginative process by which the subject, seeking to discern direction as a writer, received the message and the attachment was a powerful gift to his developing sense of vocation.

It would be easy to dismiss this as some sort of self-delusional project, but the participants will tell you differently. They have been awakened in ways they never dreamed possible; they have found new careers, new forms and depth of faith, new joy, and even of course at times a troubling question or concern.

The key is not just having the imaginative encounter but also sharing it with the group (or the spiritual director in a solo situation). Then, this sharing can touch others and may lead to some open-ended questions by others, or later, even months or years later, a dawning awareness of a truth that had been just beyond reach.

The sharing is done within some parameters; there is a structure to the time spent, including intentional quiet time and guidelines for asking questions and making comments that are nondirective and nonjudgmental so that the person sharing the imaginative experience feels safe in being open. Archer provides helpful outlines for the group process, even language to use consistently week by week that will help group members grow in trust and strength. Someone wishing to start such a group in their community will find ample resources here—and despite Archer's history of working with groups of women, these resources could certainly be used in either mixed-gender or male-only settings.

Thus, this is both an eminently creative book, offering real openness to opportunities to experience God more intimately, boldly, and imaginatively than is often the case, and a wonderful practical guide to learning just how creative and lively the Creator and we can be, especially with each other and with God.

Rev. Dr. Robin Hawley Gorsline
(he, him; they, them)
Poet*Queer Theologian

PREFACE

"Is this silly? Is this unrealistic? The age of revelation is over, you know. Are people letting their imaginations run away with them?"

"Imagining myself in the scripture introduced me to a whole new way of encountering God. *Sharing the experience* with others was a stretch for me, but the Spirit moved me in unexpected ways."

"We could go through that doorway of imagination and see where God was calling us. It felt exactly the opposite from therapy; it was not going down to analyze the hard places in our lives; it was being allowed to have wings and just go!"

These quotes are from participants in the meditative process I've come to call "shared imagination." It's the term I use to convey how one's own imagination can combine in meditation with that of the Holy One to produce not the literal "Word of God" but a synthesis of human and divine ideas. When these ideas are tested for the "fruits" to determine if they spring from and lead to Love/God, and when they are checked with trusted spiritual friends, the results can become trustworthy guideposts on the spiritual journey. Because the process I'm describing involves a person imaginatively taking part in scenes and conversations, these experiences can be much more graphic and compelling ways of encountering the Divine than is traditionally available in most church services and study groups. It can be more powerful for an individual to meet Jesus, for example, by entering a New Testament story using all five senses in imaginative meditation than by simply reading or hearing that same story. This type of prayerful, imaginative meditation is not merely fantasy, though the envisioning may have dreamlike elements and may benefit from individual and group interpretation over time. These "waking dreams" come from one's own imagination *informed* by the Holy Spirit and can constitute an encounter with the Divine. My book illustrates how this underused connection to God can function in beautiful, surprising ways.

My idea of "shared imagination" sprang directly from participating in a group format that I think is quite unique—a circle of people meditating together upon a single biblical story, text, or topic. My mentor and soul friend Pamela Barnett created the structure for these meetings in the 1980s and based the meditation portion on the imaginative envisioning that Ignatius of Loyola, founder of the Jesuit order, invented in the sixteenth century.[1] Ignatius's method of entering a Bible passage was to visualize becoming a participant or bystander in the event and letting the story unfold as it will in one's mind.[2]

The "shared imagination" process also shares fascinating elements with Carl Jung's concepts of the collective unconscious and active imagination,[3] as well as with dream interpretation methods.[4], [5] Those similarities, explained in this text, could provide an entryway into this process for people of differing faith traditions or no faith tradition. This book is rooted in my own faith of Christianity, but I believe that this imaginative method can open a channel for growth and healing, whether one labels the "other" as God, Higher Power, one's deepest self, or simply the Universe.

In our own initial group meetings, we members were helped to relax from our toes up and to breathe in God's light, love, strength, and healing power. We were then led to imaginatively reflect on a Bible story or passage, or a selection from another spirituality text. When the envisioning time was over, we could speak about what came

---

[1] Thomas Corbishley, SJ, translator, *The Spiritual Exercises of Saint Ignatius* (Wheathampstead, Hertfordshire, England: Anthony Clarke Books, 1973), 47–49.

[2] William A. Barry, SJ, *Finding God in All Things: A Companion to the Spiritual Exercises of St Ignatius* (Notre Dame, Indian: Ave Maria Press, 1991), 77–87.

[3] C.G. Jung, *The Red Book: Liber Novus, A Reader's Edition*, Sonu Shamdasani editor (NY: W.W. Norton & Company, 2009), 28, 50, 52.

[4] The Rev. Robert L. Haden Jr., *Unopened Letters from God: A Workbook for Individuals and Groups* (Haden Institute Publishing, 2010), 3.

[5] Gayle Delaney, PhD, *The Dream Kit: An All-in-One Toolkit for Understanding Your Dreams* (HarperSanFrancisco, 1995), 11–25.

up in our meditation and how it might relate to our lives at the time. Sharing one's own contemplation and life events was totally voluntary, not mandatory. The other members of the circle could gently suggest ideas about another person's meditation. We could talk about anything in our lives, and we could set aside anyone else's comments if they did not resonate with our own feelings about our life and meditation. All our conversations were to stay in that spiritual direction room, for confidentiality. Our shepherdess, Pamela, lightly guided us with ideas she had gleaned in seminary, in her reading, and in her life—always relating our meditations and our life moments back to God in lovingly gentle ways. We ended with a close-of-day prayer service.[6]

The process also included "testing the fruits and the spirits"—noticing if one is led to more (or less) love of others, self, and God—and discerning that only those meditative thoughts encompassing love, compassion, consolation, hope, and joy are from the Divine Spirit. Checking with trusted others about what came in imagination was essential, too, to help avoid self-delusion.

Shared imagination thus also involves sharing with others—the horizontal line of connection in this process. I almost titled this text *Will You Believe I'm Talking to You?* from my meditation involving the book's cover image. (Skip ahead to the chapter "A Red Velvet Pillow—With Tassels!" to read that memorable conversation with the Holy One.) That question from God in my walking meditation is a punchier title, to be sure, but it only describes the vertical connecting line in this imaginative method—the channel with God. I have found the erupting of imagination through this process to be amazing in both directions—with the Holy One and with each other! Over the years, I've experienced shared imagination spilling out into dreams, shared stories with others, imaginative conversations with God, imaginative letters I've written to holy people of the past, sudden inspiration for creative works, and some almost mystical walking and driving conversations with the Divine. Others who have experienced this shared imagination method have told me similar stories of encounters with the Holy One—in

---

[6] *The Book of Common Prayer, according to the use of The Episcopal Church* (The Church Hymnal Corporation and Seabury Press, 1977), 127.

meditations and in life events. I tell many of those stories, used with permission. Although my long-term groups have self-selected into being all-women gatherings, I have included some men's tales in this work, from combined-gender groups at conferences and retreats.

I am deeply indebted to everyone who agreed to let me publish their stories. The very power of this type of envisioning encounter with the Divine and each other is exactly in the *personal details* of those stories, those meetings in the mind with the Holy One and with soul friends. Generalizing those experiences or paraphrasing the details would never give that immediate, heartfelt impact of hearing *actual stories* told by *real people* in *their own words*. You, the reader, are experiencing shared imagination as you peruse these stories. *You* are sharing imagination with God and with these persons as you hear their tales. I cannot thank my story contributors enough for their courage and generosity in offering a glimpse into this transforming, experiential method of meeting God. I hope that you will find yourself resonating with many of these encounters and that this dip into the world of Spirit and imagination will inspire you to open for yourself this wonderful, surprise-filled channel with the Divine.

BEGINNINGS

HOW I STARTED

When I went to church that Sunday, I never dreamed my life would be altered, but interestingly, the change did not happen *during* the religious service. The transformation began, although I was barely aware of it at the time, in a conversation with a wonderful woman friend *after* the church service. That combination of belonging to a church and yet finding a closer connection to the Divine through personal, spiritual interactions has become a constant element of my journey.

I have felt for decades that I stand both inside and outside traditional religion. This borderland is the only place I can be, but it can feel countercultural and a bit isolating. In church, as I hear prayers, preaching, and hymns, I am often agreeing and disagreeing in my head, thinking, *Hmm, yes, but* … Both outside and inside church, I must choose carefully with whom I share my experiences of the Divine since there are people who would peg me as crazy or arrogant to think that the Holy One would even deign to bring experiences to me. But I'm getting ahead of myself. Let me tell you how it started that Sunday so many years ago.

I was speaking after church with Emily, a dear friend in the choir, who started describing her latest experience in a new church gathering called simply "the spiritual direction group." Everyone in the group had been encouraged one evening to ask in meditation for help with some personal goal they were trying to achieve. Emily told me that she was trying to lose weight. She described her meditation. "And then, in my mind, I saw all these helping hands reaching out to me, supporting me in my journey,"

Wow, I thought, *people* see *things at these meetings? I have to try this!*

3

So I went to the very next Monday night meeting. There, even though I had never meditated before, I responded to the instructions of the group leader, Pamela, and dutifully closed my eyes. I was immediately struck by a sense of a holy, spiritual power that seemed present in the room. It was as if I had opened a door inside myself to an *immense* space that had always been there but I had never known about. Both that inner room and the physical room in which I was sitting seemed filled with something powerful, something with substance, something like a thickness in the air. I think of that immense space now as "the universe of imagination" and that substance as "spirit."

On that first evening, as instructed, I put myself imaginatively into the suggested Bible story and spoke to God in my mind, heart, and imagination. To my complete surprise, I heard words coming back to me. I began to see images and to take part in unfolding scenes. I remember worrying that I must really have an overactive imagination and that none of this could possibly be from God. However, during the time after meditation, our shepherdess, Pamela, spoke as if she truly believed that the Divine One was speaking with each of us in our contemplations, and she somehow related all our comments—both about our meditation and about our lives—back to God. She didn't preach, she didn't tell us what to do or think, she didn't even say "God" that often, but she spoke as if our thoughts in meditation and the mundane happenings of our everyday lives were important to the Holy One.

I was so excited! I was in my late thirties and had been a churchgoer all my life, but I had never felt connected to God outside Sunday services. I had never imagined a Holy One who cared about every little aspect of my life and of everyone else's life. However, after that first meeting and meditation, I felt as if I had finally found a spiritual home. Years earlier, I had found my *musical* home inside the amazing, enveloping sound of an orchestra. Now there was another, *spiritual* world waiting to envelop me. Like the line from the Broadway musical that says, "Fish gotta swim and birds gotta fly,"[7] I knew I had to swim and fly in that dense air of spirit and imagination. I was meant to exist in that space. It was my native land.

---

[7] "Can't Help Lovin' Dat Man," *Show Boat*, music by Jerome Kern, lyrics by Oscar Hammerstein II, 1927, based on Edna Ferber's novel *Show Boat*, 1926.

It's nice to feel so sure of all that right now in my life. Back then, some thirty years ago, I felt a mixture of excitement and doubt. I worried for quite a while that what came to me in meditation was only the result of stray firings of my overwrought brain cells. It took quite a few meetings and meditations, probably a year or so, before I was convinced that what was happening to me was really shared imagination. I was envisioning with the Divine.

With Pamela's gentle guidance, I gradually became convinced that my meditations and those of all the group members were a synthesis of individual imagination with God's imagination. Experiencing and believing in that process changed my life. I not only received spiritual scenes and the group members' gentle comments to ponder over time, but I also heard the other participants' wondrous visual images, which I could hold silently in my heart as additional touchstones of the Holy One. Over time, this envisioning process branched out for our group members in ways that might have seemed crazy at the beginning but became for us amazing signposts on our spiritual journeys.

How did such a life-changing group begin? The following tale will describe the unlikely and inauspicious start of Pamela's three-part meeting format.

"OUT OF THIN AIR AND BY THE HOLY SPIRIT"

"Out of thin air and by the Holy Spirit" is how Pamela Barnett explained the genesis of the spiritual meetings that she started and where I first experienced shared imagination. Pamela and I were dear friends at church, and she was pursuing a master's degree in spiritual direction from a nearby seminary. At our church governing board meeting, she was asked to organize and lead spiritual direction meetings. Later, she told me how she "fell into" inventing a group format.

"This was purely out of thin air and by the Holy Spirit as far as I was concerned," Pamela confessed to me. "I didn't know what the heck I was doing! I knew about *individual* spiritual direction, but I didn't know anything about *group* work. I had a vague idea of how I would structure the meetings, I guess. I didn't know much about meditation at that point, but I did know I wanted a meditation time, and then discussion, and then end with Compline[8] (a close-of-day prayer service)."

Emily, my choir friend who later interested me in coming to the gatherings, remembered being at that board meeting where the group format was first discussed.

"I asked Pamela what spiritual direction was," Emily told me. "Pamela replied that it was sitting down one-on-one with someone and helping that person understand his or her relationship with God. I was intimidated at the thought that I would have to sit down with one person and try to talk about my relationship with God. I didn't know if I even had a relationship with the Divine. I went to church, I

---

[8] *The Book of Common Prayer, according to the use of the Episcopal Church* (The Church Hymnal Corporation and Seabury Press, 1977), 127.

had what I considered a faith, but I wasn't on any particular journey. I certainly didn't understand the words *spirituality* or *religiosity*. Those terms were confused in my mind. But I had experience in group work based on the principles of Alcoholics Anonymous. I was used to being in a collective gathering where people shared their own stories and where we knew that whatever was said in the room stayed in the room. I was comfortable in that milieu of a confidential trust relationship. So I told Pamela that I thought spiritual direction would be easier in a group. She replied that she thought that would be dreadful!"

Emily laughingly continued. "But then Pamela said, 'Well, I don't know how that would work, but why don't we have a meeting?' So we did."

What a seemingly accidental beginning for a group format that has deeply affected so many lives! The Holy Spirit truly must have been at work.

Initially, the meetings were open to both women and men, but after nearly a year of very few men showing up, Pamela decided to officially make the group an all-woman gathering, renaming it the Women's Spiritual Direction Group.

Emily explained that shift to me. "At the first organizational meeting, quite a few men came, as well as women. The men wanted to base the meetings on a book or a case study. They seemed comfortable with that because it was factual. The women who showed up didn't seem interested in that direction, and Pamela suggested that we base the meetings on meditation." Chuckling, Emily continued her tale. "At one meeting when it was still open to both genders, a man came to the meeting and threw us women off because he was uncomfortable with the lengthening quiet time we women had grown accustomed to and had learned to even enjoy."

I suspect it was pretty uncomfortable for that lone male also! I have used meditation with men in individual spiritual direction and in mixed-gender groups at retreats and conferences. Men are quite capable of using imagination in meditation and discussing their own deep, spiritual lives. However, all my long-term gatherings have eventually self-selected into being all-women, probably because I'm a woman and because there may be an increased ease of sharing in single-gender groups.

Under Pamela's shepherding, the initial group added specific practices to her three-part format of meditation, discussion, and prayer. She helped us women focus on becoming quiet by sometimes having us enter the room in complete silence. On other occasions, she would begin by going around the circle and asking each woman to briefly describe how she was feeling that night. Pamela invented a method of helping us relax our bodies from our toes up while breathing in God's "light, love, strength, and healing power," and then breathing out to God "all worries, cares and burdens, all things to get done, and all things we wish we had not done." I still light a candle, as Pamela did, and then use the following relaxation talk and physical guidelines for becoming receptive during the quiet period. The talk alternates between consciously relaxing parts of the body and breathing in God's love and power.

Relaxation Talk

Find a comfortable spot in the chair or on the sofa, with your hands open and receptive and your feet resting easily on the floor. With your eyes closed, begin to scan your body for any tension, tightness, or dis-ease. Beginning at your feet, flex and relax the muscles in your toes, the arches of your feet, your ankles. Let go of any tightness in the calves of your legs; relax any tension in your thighs and let your stomach muscles just go slack. Begin to take in a few deep breaths, and as you inhale, breathe in God's light and love, God's strength and healing power. As you breathe out, imagine surrounding yourself with that light, love, and healing power, much as the candle flame on our table is surrounded by light.

Feel the chair or sofa supporting your back. Relax the muscles in your shoulders. Release any tension in the muscles of your upper arms, your lower arms, your palms and fingers. Feel any tightness flowing out the tips of your fingers. Breathe in God's light, love, strength, and healing power. Breathe out all things that seem heavy or burdensome. Hand over to God all cares, worries, and responsibilities, things that need to be done and things we wish we had not done. Let God hold all those things during these moments, so that we don't have to.

Let go of any tension in your neck and jaw. Release any tightness around your mouth and around your eyes. Imagine you can even relax behind your eyes. Let your forehead smooth out and picture all the rest of the tension in your body flowing out the top of your head. One more time, breathe in God's light, unconditional love, and power to heal whatever needs healing in you this very evening. As you exhale, breathe out the things of yesterday, today, and tomorrow, so that we might meet God in God's eternal now, where only these moments matter.

This relaxation talk is also extremely important in anchoring the group's meditations in God. Breathing in the Holy One's light, love, strength, and healing power not only infuses each member with God's Spirit but also keeps the meditations grounded in the Divine. When I first joined the group, I worried about whether my imagination might take me into unsafe spiritual waters. That worry subsided over time as I noticed that my meditations (and those of the other women) were positive and reassuring—almost never frightening. Pamela counseled us to look squarely at anything that <u>did seem</u> unsettling in our meditations, to see if that thing would change to something more positive. She also instructed us to ask any frightening thought or image, "Is that really you, Jesus?" Untrustworthy spirits flee from that question, she said. For a more detailed description of Ignatius's discernment of spirits, see the chapter "Testing the Fruits and Spirits, Checking with Others" later in this book.

With time, experience, and wise counseling from our shepherdess, Pamela, I felt quite safe letting my imagination go in meditations. I came to "see" in my mind's eye Jesus as an anchor in the middle of the room, with all of us attached to him by lengths of light beams. We could not go too far afield in our thoughts and imaginings, because we were connected to Jesus.

For meditation topics, Pamela brought in stories from the Bible as well as meditations from books on spirituality she was reading. (See Appendix B: Meditation Topics, for helpful books.) Once we had closed our eyes and gone through Pamela's relax-and-breathe-in-God exercise, she would read us the Bible story or meditation, which we would enter imaginatively that evening.

Pamela used the method that was invented in the sixteenth century by Ignatius of Loyola (founder of the Jesuit order) of entering a meditation in imagination.[9] To help us use all our five senses in imagination, Pamela would ask questions like, "What does the landscape look like?" "How does the weather feel—hot, dry, and dusty, or cloudy, rainy, and damp?" Can you hear any sounds, perhaps people speaking or birds singing?" "Are there any smells you notice?" "What does Jesus (or Mary, or a disciple, or a person in the crowd) look like?" "Look down at your feet and notice what type of shoes you are wearing." "What does your clothing feel like against your skin?" "If you are at the seaside, can you taste the tang of saltwater in the air?" "If you are eating a meal, what flavors do you experience?" Then Pamela would leave us in silence to let the story or meditation play out in our minds however it would.

After the quiet time—at the first meetings this lasted only a few minutes but increased as the group became accustomed to meditating—Pamela would bring us out of the quiet by saying, "And when you're completely ready, I invite you to wrap up your meditation, open your eyes, and become present in this room again." Then she would ask, "How did that time go for any of you?" She would wait, staring patiently at the pattern of the carpet, until a woman felt like sharing what had come up for her during the quiet time.

After someone spoke, Pamela modeled the nondirective way we could speak to each other, something she called "talking across the circle." By her example and directions, our shepherdess encouraged us to ask gentle questions about another person's meditation and make open-ended suggestions on what a meditation image might mean. We

---

[9] William A. Barry, SJ, *Finding God in All Things: A Companion to the Spiritual Exercises of St Ignatius* (Notre Dame, Indian: Ave Maria Press, 1991), 77–87.

were guided to avoid using the word "should" when speaking to another person or when talking about ourselves. And *always* Pamela encouraged us to check within ourselves to see if another person's comments to us resonated with our deepest self or not. Comments that did not resonate inside us, no matter how gentle the comment or how well-meaning, could be simply disregarded.

I learned much later, in other confidential group settings, that talking directly to another person is often not allowed. In those meeting formats, this type of speaking is negatively called "cross-talk" and is forbidden to avoid anyone giving advice or commenting on the validity of another person's sharing. Avoiding cross-talk is a blessing in many groups I attend. However, it was also a blessing to be able to talk "across the circle" in these spiritual direction meetings, using the gentle, nondirective ways into which Pamela guided us. My own encapsulation of those discussion guidelines can be found in Appendix A: Aids for Meetings in this book.

During the discussion period, Pamela often explained "testing the fruits" of meditation, by urging us to test over time whether our thoughts and experiences during a meditation brought us to more love of God, neighbor, and self, or led us to less love. Only those ideas and insights that led to more love were to be trusted. Toward the end of this discussion time, she would explain "Holy Forgetting"[10]—a term coined by spiritual writer/teacher Margaret Guenther—where whatever was said by another member of the group that night was forgotten (kept completely confidential) when we left the meeting room.

Can you imagine a more gentle, safe, inviting soil in which to grow spiritually? Through this process, God was tenderly inviting us and genuinely interested in us. It was no wonder that this original group met every single Monday night, steadily, for just over six years. The group method evolved and changed slightly over time, but Pamela's tender guidance toward the Divine remained the constant element. With her deep spirituality, calm presence, and self-deprecating humor, Pamela led us on paths of self-discovery and Divine discovery in gentle,

---

[10] Margaret Guenther, *Holy Listening: The Art of Spiritual Direction* (Cambridge, MA: Cowley Publications, 1992), 30, 19.

insightful ways. Our excitement at encountering the Holy in this gentle, imagination-filled way was tremendous.

Why did this process seem counter to my previous experiences in the Christian religion? For one thing, the scope of what we could talk about was boundless in the group. We did not limit ourselves to speaking only about our prayer life or about holy topics. Pamela never told us directly that we could bring up any topic we wanted to; she simply listened intensely and intuitively to anything we said. Somehow, she could always relate our meditations and our lives to the Holy. I was amazed that God cared about the mundane details of our lives. That concept somehow never seemed to find me during the decades of church services I had attended before coming to the spiritual direction group.

Most importantly, the group was led by a *non-clergy woman*, Pamela. That element was so important in my openness to growing spiritually. I remember trying out Bible study classes when I was a young adult. I disliked them intensely, because they always seemed to devolve into a male minister telling the rest of us exactly what a scripture passage meant. There was no chance in those Bible study classes to experience the Divine personally in imagination or to interpret scripture or one's own experience for one's self.

Contrary to that process, in the spiritual direction group, we women had a more direct encounter with God through shared imagination. We could then share with each other. As each woman described her meditation and her life, we could imagine what her contemplative images might mean if they were ours. We could intuit our way into the thoughts and lives of the other members of the group, with gentle comments that could be discarded if they did not resonate with that woman. Each of us could feel our way toward interpretations of our meditations with the help of other non-ordained women, always gently guided by our layperson shepherdess. Our experiences of God did not need to be channeled through someone who was ordained or through a man.

That the group was all women was incredibly nurturing for me. Feminism was certainly alive in the late 1980s, when I began coming to those meetings, but it had not entered my church experience at all. Only men were ordained; they led the churches, they interpreted scripture, and they were "*the* authority" on all holy matters. However, in this gathering, God spoke to and through women. We were on a journey of exploring our inner selves and discovering more about the Divine without any male supervision. Imagine that!

MEDITATION STORIES AND MEETING STRUCTURE

COLLECTING THE STORIES

After attending this original Women's Spiritual Direction Group for about nine years, I decided to pursue the same master's degree in spiritual direction that Pamela had obtained at General Theological Seminary in New York City.

For six years, I attended the seminary part-time, taking academic and experiential classes during the three-week sessions in June called "Summers at General," and attending 8:30 a.m. classes during the fall, winter, and spring. From those early morning classes, I would hop into my car and rush uptown to the Metropolitan Opera House for the 11 a.m. orchestra rehearsals. I loved my time at the seminary as much as I loved playing in that orchestra!

For my master's thesis at the seminary, I decided to create a history of our church's Women's Spiritual Direction Group, its methods, and its outcomes for individual women. I interviewed the women who were willing to let me record their stories, outside of the meetings, on tape. I used few cues, simply asking what they valued in the group experience and where they might have been led in their lives because of the gatherings. I did ask if they would be willing to share any individual meditations that seemed especially important or memorable.

I transcribed the recorded interviews, often while I sat in the women's locker room at the Metropolitan Opera House between the daytime rehearsals and the evening performances. I loved transcribing the stories of the women in the group, and I tried to keep their individual voices in my transcriptions. To me, their encounters with the Divine were the gleaming, golden value of these imagination-filled meditative gatherings. The women talked about everything from individual meditations to the welcoming atmosphere in the gathering room, to the inner and outer changes they noticed in themselves because of their attendance at the meetings. I was amazed at how six or seven hours of transcribing these tapes would fly by without my noticing the time. As women musicians began arriving in the locker room for the evening performance, I would be startled to see that so many hours had gone by.

Once I had typed up the women's tales, with only slight changes to clean up grammar and hesitations, I made copies of each woman's sharing, showed them to each individual, and obtained each one's permission to include their words in my thesis. Not everyone who spoke with me gave permission, and I respected their wishes and did not use their stories. At the completion of the process, I destroyed the tapes.

After graduation from seminary, I hoped to craft my thesis into a publishable book, but after some nibbles of interest from publishers and then three rejections within one devastating week, I lost heart and put the project away for fourteen years. A writing course I took in 2015 renewed my enthusiasm to write a memoir/instructional book about this group process. For this present book, I have included a few men's stories (from private spiritual direction or combined-gender groups) and have submitted or resubmitted my written version of each person's sharing to that individual, asking for written and dated permission to use the accounts in a published book. I keep a notebook of the printed stories and the signed and dated permission slips. Again, not everyone agreed to have her or his story published, and I have respected each one's wishes as to whether to include their stories, how they would like to change my written account, and whether to use their real names. The tales are very personal, and each contributor must be comfortable in sharing them with a wider audience. I am incredibly grateful to these narrators. When told *with permission*, their stories are the gold of this method and of this book—the closest thing to experiencing one's own imaginative meeting with God or hearing of another's in a group. Thank you, my dear friends and storytellers, for sharing in this book your encounters with the Holy One.

THE MEETING ROOM

The best type of room for these meditation meetings has comfortable, upholstered furniture, eye-level lighting, soft carpeting, and, of course, a door that can be closed. Most churches have a parlor that fits this description—a place that looks like a cross between a living room and a library. In one church where I've led this type of group, I was encouraged to use a classroom with long tables, overhead lights, hard chairs, and bare floors. When I expressed my concerns about that room, it was suggested that I use a library setting *that had no doors to close!* I politely held out for the church's parlor. A classroom atmosphere or any space without a door is *not* conducive to meditating and speaking about very private experiences.

Sarah, our musical member, described to me what she loved about the space where our original group held our gatherings. At her initial meeting, she found herself the first person to arrive that evening. "When I came into the room," she told me, "and being there alone for a while, I was very struck by the *presence* the room had even without anybody being in there. I was very taken with that. It felt very quiet and calm, and a place where people came to be quiet and calm. Do you know how a space feels when it's tended in a certain way? It's like when somebody cares for it to keep it available for its function."

Elaborating on her subject, Sarah continued, "It's like when a kitchen is kept in really good working order so that you can cook, easily and often and fancifully. The larder is stocked, the refrigerator is clean and full, and the dish drainer is empty, so you can really get in there and do your stuff. That room felt tended in that same way for quiet time. There were all these books around about prayer. It was cozy. It was small. The lighting was good. It just felt peaceful and so tucked away. It wasn't near the other offices, it was right nestled up against the chancel of our church, and that felt like a really nice place to be. That felt good."

Our artistic member, Sharon, felt that the room had become a comfortable yet powerful place because of the meditating and confidential sharing that took place in our meetings. She explained to me, "The room itself is such a comfortable and safe place. It's very quiet, but at the same time, there is a power that seems to be here when the group is gathered, and sometimes even when it's not. It's as if there are vibrations that linger behind."

The seating arrangement is also very important. In this group format, all the members should sit more or less in a circle—a vital aspect of the group dynamic. A circle feels less like a committee meeting and less like a teacher-student relationship. Women especially seem to gravitate toward circle-shaped gatherings, partly because of their lack of hierarchy. Although there is an acknowledged leader/facilitator in this meeting structure, the circle form makes conversation seem more between equals, an important feeling in these meetings.

Lesley Northup, in her book *Ritualizing Women*, has much to say about using a circle as a form for women's gatherings. "Few images encapsulate the spirit of women's ritualizing as effectively as the circle, and few women's rituals are conducted in any other arrangement. ... Such a configuration also makes it possible for ritual participants to most fully interact with one another."[11]

Later in her book, Northup writes, "The extension of circularity is horizontality, through which women's ritualizing is liberated from the excessive verticality typical of male-focused religion. Women's ritual actions tend to be grounded, nonhierarchical, spreading, and community centered. Perhaps one of the most hierarchical of all religious symbols is the (high) priest, a person perceived as set apart for special meditation of the divine. Most women' rituals consciously subvert such

---

[11] Lesley A. Northup, *Ritualizing Women: Patterns of Spirituality* (Cleveland, Ohio: The Pilgrim Press, 1997), 29–30.

hierarchical leadership roles in favor of an egalitarian and horizontal model or rotating, shared, or minimized leadership."[12]

Though Northup is writing about *ritual* space, and this group meeting model is not a sacred *service* of the church, nevertheless, these gatherings are a time of meeting the Divine through silence and shared conversation, so I believe that Northup's comments hold true. The circle shape is very important for sharing stories, as well as for putting less emphasis on one high, exalted, holier-than-the-rest-of-us leader. There *is* one leader in this group format, but that facilitator operates like a spiritual director, with the members acting as spiritual friends to each other. I quote Pamela's words on this diluted sense of hierarchy in the later chapter of this book called "Good Shepherding Qualities."

---

[12] Lesley A. Northup, *Ritualizing Women: Patterns of Spirituality* (Cleveland, Ohio: The Pilgrim Press, 1997), 59.

SHOWING UP

What made the women of this group come to their first meeting? How did they feel when they arrived? What made them come back and become regular members? The answers to those questions have differences as well as similarities, as you might expect from a group of diverse women who were coming for a common purpose.

It seems that for almost everyone, a personal invitation or personal comment propelled them to their first meeting. Sarah and I both recall quite clearly the moment she became interested in our group.

"I was sitting with you, Mary Ann," Sarah began, "in the back row of the sopranos in the church choir. I saw you checking this little box on the 'Time and Talent Pledge Sheet'[13] that said 'Women's Spiritual Direction Group.' It wasn't even two seconds past when you got your pen through that little mark when I asked you what that was. It was in the middle of a church service—not really an opportune time to have a lengthy conversation about what this group was all about. However, you said something that was enough to pique my curiosity."

Sarah went on, "The invitation to join the group came at a point in my life when I was really able to receive that offer for a number of reasons. I was relatively new to the community, feeling alienated by all sorts of things (although feeling very welcomed in the choir). It was nice to have some reason to be connected to this town where I had come for my husband's job—but where I felt little or no connection. I don't remember how much longer it was after that Sunday that I first came to

---

[13] This is an often-used, variously worded handout in church services that asks parishioners to pledge not only money but also their time and their special talents in service to God and the church.

the group, but not too long. I was *ready* and *hungry*. I had lots of energy to bring to your description of a group of women who get together, meditate, and talk about their meditations and their lives, and who end saying Compline prayer."[14]

Melinda, our earthy comedienne, joined the group at its very first meeting and soon invited two other women. The opposite responses she received from her verbal invitations illustrate how this gathering can feel just right for some women but not for others. She laughed as she began her story. "I remember that Susan started within the first few months of the group because I called and invited her. I also called Diana, who said, 'Well, I'm so busy, I have so much to do, etcetera.' I said, 'Look, Diana, this is not about anything like *bringing a cake*. This is not about *scheduling an event*. Here, you come, and be yourself, and meditate, and pray. It's just great, really nurturing for your spirituality.' Diana said, 'Oh well, no thanks.' But when I had said the same things to Susan, she had responded, 'You know, that sounds interesting.'"

For Donna, our member who later became a priest, it was the advice of two other women priests who were running a retreat that gave her the impetus to come to our gatherings. She related her story to me, "The spiritual direction group had been part of our church here for a long time, but even though I kept reading about it, the idea didn't click yet in my mind. It was when I went on my first-ever retreat that I thought about spiritual direction. The two women who led the retreat made two suggestions to me. One was that I find a spiritual director. The other was that I start a program called Education for Ministry. When I came back home after that retreat, finally it went across my radar screen, that, son of a gun, *our church had a spiritual direction group!* So, I came."

What propelled Sharon, an art lecturer, to first come to our meetings was an emotional crisis. Yet, even in her case, it was a personal conversation that precipitated her initial visit to our gathering. She explained, "I think I had been coming to our church here for three or four years, and I knew about the spiritual direction group but had not really thought about it seriously for *me*. I knew about it, but I had dismissed it as 'not my thing' or not something that I would be involved

---

[14] *The Book of Common Prayer, according to the use of The Episcopal Church* (The Church Hymnal Corporation and Seabury Press, 1977), 127.

in. I forgot about it entirely for a number of years. Then, I experienced a crisis in my life. I went to talk with our rector about this quandary that I was in. Our priest said that what had happened was a wake-up call. I was really struggling with what I was supposed to wake up to and what I was supposed to do with it. There was the possibility of great harm in what I was struggling with. The rector here suggested that coming to this women's group might help me. That's what got me here, to spiritual direction."

What kept us women coming back to meetings? What kept us showing up? For me, it was the surprise and joy of directly experiencing God through meditational images and thoughts. It was the delight and wonder of experiencing a Holy One who was actually concerned about our everyday lives. Perhaps most importantly, no matter how tired I was at the beginning of meetings, I left our gatherings with a sense of lightness, refreshment, and peace. Those feelings propelled me to come to each following meeting.

For Sarah, our opera singer, continuing to show up helped her become more comfortable conversing with and about God. She explained, "I think I liked the idea before I came of talking about my spiritual life. That's not something that I had been in the habit of separating out from the other parts, like the psychological, the emotional, the relational, the career, etcetera. That spiritual part was interesting to me. I also liked the idea of being a community of people meditating together rather than meditating alone. That appealed to me very much. But I was scared to be sitting around in a room and talking about God, to be perfectly honest. I was scared because I'm not a professional God-person; I'm not a priest. I also have felt my whole life that I have wanted to have more conversation on a regular basis about God and with God but have not taken that opportunity. I felt sort of silly sometimes, embarrassed, shy, like being in a new, fledgling relationship, a vulnerable relationship that is difficult to enter into and go out of if one is not habituated to that new connection. I think part of the gift of this group is that conversing with God and about God becomes part of the rhythm and the habit of the normal fabric of day-to-day, week-to-week life."

Melinda believes that the discipline of showing up for meetings helped her bring her inner beliefs and insights into her outer life-in-the-world.

She explained, "I remember an insight, a new idea that came to me one night at the meeting. I was just beginning to feel within myself that I was divided, that I was giving power to a voice inside myself that said what I imagined my artist friends and critics were saying to me, 'Have kids?—a trap. Believe in God?—a numbing for your mind.' And this voice was reinforced by my father's voice, which said the same negative things about belief in God. This was the first time I realized I was giving power to those negative voices inside me. Often, I'd come here to the group meeting and feel perfectly safe and be able to pray and talk about my spiritual life and get insights like this one.

"But," Melinda continued, "then I'd leave the room and I would think, *Okay, that's all just in this room.* My spiritual life and my everyday life were very compartmentalized for me. Even when I see old notations in my journal that make me say, 'Wow, that's very insightful,' I look back on my life and think, *But how far did that insight travel out of this room after that?* I have to say that sometimes it didn't travel very far. Insights can be a dime a dozen."

Summing up, this spiritual and honest woman told me, "However, because Pamela was very faithful at keeping the group going—never failing to show up just because she may have felt tired or had her own problems—a person like me could come enough times so that these insights could be reinforced. I could have a safe place to practice being a Christian, practice thinking about Jesus, practice opening my spiritual self, so that eventually I had enough of a foundation so that I could bring my spiritual self out into the rest of the world. That discipline of showing up enough was absolutely invaluable."

VIVID IMAGININGS

Because we women were encouraged to use all five senses in imagination during the meditation time, we often had very intense scenes and feelings come to us. I'd like to share three women's meditations, which contain that aspect of rich sensual imagining.

The first tale is of the time Emily experienced the physical sensation of feet walking down the church aisle in one of her most graphic contemplations. Emily began her story. "It was on a very, very, very hot night. It was so sweltering in our meeting room that Pamela said we could go anywhere comfortable in the church itself. She would keep the lights off in the church to make it a little cooler. I remember lying down on the center aisle carpet on the way up to the altar, at the front pews. I was lying spread eagle there, just relaxing, cooling off; trying to let go and get deeper into a meditation. I became aware of feet—and I don't just mean shined-up, dressed-up shoes. I felt all kinds of shoes, and sandals, and bare feet. I was aware of millions of people who had walked this walk to the altar of Christ. And I just was overcome by it. I felt like a small little pinprick in this huge mass of humanity. It was an awesome experience."

Continuing, Emily told me, "Then I remembered that I had the same feeling at a Christian education conference hearing Herbert O'Driscoll[15] speak on the words in the Episcopal service, 'Christ has died. Christ is risen. Christ will come again.' O'Driscoll stood on his tiptoes and reached to his right and said, 'We look over the millennia of years and millions of heads to the cross, and say, "*Christ has died.*"'

---

[15] Dean of New Westminster, Vancouver, Canada, 1968–1982.

Then he turned to us and put his hands across his chest to indicate that Christ was within him and said, '*Christ is risen.*' Then he turned to his left, reached again, opening his hands as though to pass that Spirit on to others, and said, '*Christ will come again.*'[16] And during that meditation while I was lying in the church aisle, I had that same feeling of multitudes of people who had walked the path of faith to Christ. It was very powerful. It was awesome. It was sort of an overwhelming experience, like being swept up in a great force."

Years later, I interviewed Emily again about that meditative experience. She recalled, "I was flooded with the idea that life is all about that truth—the Spirit was within faithful people in the past, and now is in me, and will be in God's people in the future. That's how I'm going to see the Holy Spirit. And I do feel as though I never question that the Spirit is within me, that God is within me, if I only listen. And in those mornings when I wonder what the day will bring, I'm ready for anything if I just stop for a minute and say, '*Yes God, I know You're with me.*' It was a life-changing moment that I still carry now, many years later. Every Sunday when we say, 'Christ has died. Christ is risen. Christ will come again,' I find that I have to open my hands, as a way of opening my eyes and heart to feel the Holy Spirit within me."

Sarah, one of our younger members and an opera singer, seemed to use all her imaginative senses in two particularly memorable meditations.

Sarah began her first story. "In one meditation, I was talking with Jesus in a church in New Mexico, a deeply spiritual place for me, and Jesus was speaking to me in Spanish. It smelled like orange blossoms. It was a very sensual experience. Jesus was sitting behind me and called me *mi hija*, 'my daughter.' It was lovely."

The second meditation centered on the Bible story of the Transfiguration, where Jesus took three disciples—Peter, James, and John—to the top of a mountain to pray. On the mountaintop, the disciples witnessed Jesus become dazzling white and speak to the long-dead Jewish spiritual leaders Moses and Elijah. All three disciples were amazed and frightened, but Peter, often the most talkative of Jesus's

---

[16] *The Book of Common Prayer, according to the use of The Episcopal Church* (The Church Hymnal Corporation and Seabury Press, 1977), 363.

followers, rambled on about how they should build three booths or tents on that mountaintop—one each for Jesus, Moses, and Elijah. Suddenly a cloud covered all of them, and a voice from the cloud announced, "This is my Son, my Beloved. Listen to him." When the disciples looked again, they saw only Jesus (Matthew 17:1–9; Mark 9:2–10; Luke 9:28–36).

Launching into her imaginative version of the story, Sarah said, "I remember the meditation about the mountaintop, the Transfiguration, where I was walking up the mountain in this multilayered costume from Mozart's time. I was gradually stripping, taking pieces of clothing off and leaving them on the bushes as I went up. I was having this wonderful experience of walking with Jesus up the mountain, seeing these 'doofuses,' the disciples, at the mountaintop trying to build tents. I remember thinking, *What are you guys doing? It's such a lovely day. The sun is shining so hard.* I had eaten an orange, and I had orange dribbling all down my chin. I had this lovely verbal interchange with Jesus. The clouds came out, but I didn't care. Then it was time to go back down the mountain. I went first. I had taken off my shoes and my stockings, just about everything, and it got difficult walking down. I got scared, and my feet started to get cuts and to bleed and have blisters. I didn't think I could do it. The going up was easy; the coming down was very, very difficult and painful. And I asked, 'Jesus, will you carry me?'

"He said, 'No, I won't, but I'll walk behind you.'"

Wrapping up, Sarah continued, "That was very powerful. Every Transfiguration Sunday, I'm still back in our meeting room, in that moment. That meditation has really, really lasted. I definitely wrote that one down in all kinds of details."

Melinda, our down-to-earth, sometimes hilariously comedic member, had quite a graphic meditation about the Bible story of the man needing healing at the Pool of Bethesda. In the Bible account, many people with illnesses were lying around a pool, which was thought to heal the first person who entered it once the water was mysteriously stirred up. Jesus asked one man who had been there for thirty-eight years why he was still there. The man answered that when the water was stirred, he couldn't get there fast enough, and no one would help him enter the water. Jesus told him to pick up his bed and walk. The man did so and was immediately healed (John 5:2–10a).

Melinda read to me her meditation version of that story from her journal. "The pool is set in the center of a marble amphitheater. The weather is hot, muggy, and sunny. The amphitheater is sunken into a closely mowed lawn behind Caulder Auditorium at Queens College. The people sitting around the pool are students. I especially note my friend Jean, who sometimes appears whole and sometimes appears as if half her body has rotted or been eaten away. I am sitting next to her, and I'm covered with grotesque rolls of fat."

Melinda broke off reading and laughed about her own appearance, "Well, that came true!"

Reading aloud, she continued, "My double chin reaches my feet. I am a pyramid of naked flesh surmounted by a head. The marble is cool. Everyone is sitting and chatting now and enjoying the dark purple water of the pool in which the clouds and sky are reflected. The sick man from the Bible story lies on his platform on a straw beach mat elevated at the head. As I get closer, I see he has AIDS. It is wasting his body. His back teeth have fallen out. White foaming fluid is dripping from the corners of his mouth."

Melinda then read to me how the miracle happened in her imaginative version of the Bible story. "Jesus is an older college student in jeans and a T-shirt and sandals, with dark curly hair and thick glasses that show magnified, sensitive eyes. I talk to the sick man to find out what I can do, but I am too heavy to move myself and him. He smells bad and is disgusting, but at the same time, I'm crying out to help him, but I'm not able. Jesus comes and holds the man's face, looks in his eyes; and where Jesus touches the man's body, his body is healed. He touches the man's gums, and his teeth come in. When the healed man stands to walk, his legs are strong, muscular, tan, and golden haired."

Finishing with some self-insight from her meditation, Melinda read, "Jesus comes to me and will wait with me *until I am ready* to go to the pool to be healed."

What graphic pictures of ugliness and disease and of Jesus's power to heal that which seems corrupted beyond repair! These stories are just a few of the examples of the vivid nature of sharing imagination with the Divine.

A FAVORITE PLACE

For people like me, who have difficulty clearing their minds for centering prayer, the shared imagination process can be a liberating joy, exactly because of its visual component. Other folks have told me how much they also cherish this pathway. Betsy confided in me, over lunch, that she had always gravitated in meditation to a specific visual scene in her mind—a bench by a lake—where she and Jesus held imagined conversations. She remembered that sometimes she sat in Jesus's lap, sometimes they sat side by side and conversed, other times she followed some item of beauty in the landscape—but always she felt drawn to that visual scene in meditation. Betsy confessed that sometimes she had felt like a failure at meditating because she could never clear her mind of thoughts or images. When she came to one of our shared imagination meetings, she took to the process like a duck to water, or like the sunlit sparkles on the lake she always imagined in her meditative scene.

I was amazed to hear the description of her favorite imaginary place because it was almost exactly like the preferred setting-in-the-mind for one of my group members from fifteen years earlier. That woman's special location was on a bench overlooking a bay in Maine, and she returned to that spot over and over again in meditation, always coming back with insightful and moving words from her conversations with Jesus.

Another woman's favorite spot was on her grandmother's lap as that older woman sat rocking in front of the fire in her house. This group member could even smell the bread baking in her favorite place to be in imagination. My own preferred imaginative spots have included being on a covered bench in my rose garden in New Jersey or on my screened porch in Virginia, overlooking an acre of mown grass. I'm sure those places spoke to me because they provided a link of beauty to locations where I had lived in the past. So many of my group members loved finding present, or remembered, or imaginary places to be in their minds that I often started meditations by inviting everyone in the circle to find that spot before talking with the Divine. It's a wonderful, simple tool to help people begin a conversation with the Holy One in meditation.

ALLAYING FEARS ABOUT MEDITATING

Not all our meditative times were filled with descriptive scenes—vivid sights, smells, tastes, sounds, thoughts, and feelings. Often the group members spoke about being unable to meditate "correctly" or being distracted during the silence. I would worry if nothing came to me in contemplation. What would I talk about in the discussion time? Pamela always shepherded us well in those times of self-doubt, even bringing in an article from *Presence: The Journal of Spiritual Directors International*, called "Distractions in Prayer: Stumbling Blocks or Stepping Stones?" by Jean Gill.[17] That article told the tale of a woman distracted in prayer by a list of things to do for an upcoming family gathering. Feeling she had failed in praying, the author then "heard" from Jesus that her list-making ability was motivated by love for her family and was one of Jesus's favorite traits about the author. Reading that article helped me immensely in feeling loved and approved of by God even when no thoughts came in meditation.

Emily described Pamela's gentle, patient assistance in helping the group members meditate. "Meditating was a skill that Pamela taught us very diligently: from the basics of placing our feet on the floor, to the sitting posture to assume: holding our hands open and receptive—everything! For those of us who might have been scared by the word 'meditate,' or had never experienced it, or who doubted ourselves, we needed that physical guidance. As one becomes more adept at meditating, you may find there is a personal way that you are

---

[17] Jean Gill, "Distractions in Prayer: Stumbling Blocks or Stepping Stones?" *Presence: The Journal of Spiritual Directors International* 3, no. 1 (January 1997): 6–18.

more comfortable sitting, or there is a certain chair you prefer, or you develop your own rhythm, and you're able to experience contemplation more your own way. *But we were novices! We had never meditated before!* And Pamela was a very helpful teacher."

Pamela also gave us permission to let go of expectations on how we should experience any given night's quiet period. She affirmed us in whatever we experienced and stressed that what had come to us was probably the very thing we needed from God that evening. Over time, the members of our meditating circle began to relax our bodies and minds during the silence, and we worried less about performing the contemplation "correctly." When I took over leadership of the group, I wrote up the following handout of Pamela's ideas on how to help allay fears concerning meditating.

Meditating

There is no wrong way to meditate! During contemplation, we may see images and hear words, or think thoughts, or go with our distractions—which are often the Holy Spirit calling us to something important! Some of us may simply sit quietly in the presence of God. A person may experience different types of imaginings at different meetings. A few of us may even fall asleep on occasion! God brings us what we need at the time—even if that is much-needed rest! We need to reassure ourselves that there is no wrong way to spend the quiet period and that whatever comes is God's gift to us for that evening.

I still remind myself and the participants in the circle of the impossibility of meditating incorrectly. We are all self-critical at times, but God invites us to join in imagining and even helps make those meditative times fruitful in just the right way for each woman. To paraphrase a medieval woman mystic, Mechthild of Magdeburg, "God has enough of all things except one. Of communion with people, God can never have enough."[18]

---

[18] Frank Tobin, *Mechthild of Magdeburg: The Flowing Light of the Godhead* (NY: Paulist Press, 1998), 153.

SHARING OUR THOUGHTS

Not only was meditating new to most of us in the circle, sharing our contemplative ideas and life stories was also different for many of us. For Donna, one of our members who went on to become a priest, sharing was pretty scary for a long time.

Sitting in our meeting room for an interview with me, she explained, "I had no idea of what spiritual direction was. So, when I started, and I first entered this room, I was pretty fearful. My anxiety level was very high. I knew the women in the room, all of them. There were no strangers there for me. But this idea of meditating in a group and then sharing that experience was very alien to me. I'd meditated since I was in my teens. I'd been taught that by a former rector's wife, who was a physician and who taught meditation as a Lenten program. So, when I came into this room, I found the space very inviting, and yet I still felt very anxious. It was a long time before I spoke in this space. I did a lot of listening."

Our fearful sharer explained the change that slowly occurred within her. "I think it took me a while before I felt safe here. As I listened to the interactions between and among the women who were present, I experienced the women and their sharing as being healthy, helpful, compassionate, and generous of spirit. It took me a while before I observed and listened and found my own space here. *It is holy space.* Of course, so is the church, but not every person who comes to church can be open, gentle, giving, compassionate, and caring. However, I found that was true of the women here. Whether we were in this room or outside this place, there was a sort of 'caringness' that even carried past our Monday night experiences."

For my own part, I found the sharing/discussion time to be as fruitful as my own meditations—and sometimes more insightful and helpful! I learned to treasure those times of gentle conversation. Pamela's guidelines for nondirective, open-ended conversation made the sharing time immensely valuable and avoided all criticism and advice giving. I incorporated our shepherdess's ideas, along with the necessity of confidentiality—Margaret Guenther's term of "Holy Forgetting"[19]—into the following handout.

ASSISTS and Holy Forgetting

Ask gentle questions.
Skip the
Shoulds.
I
Statements.
Time for
Silence.

These guidelines for discussion encourage gentleness with each other as we talk "across the circle." We may ask open-ended questions for clarification about what a person has revealed of his or her thoughts, faith, or life. We can ask questions such as, "Could God be asking or leading you to do this or that?" We avoid all statements such as "you should, "you will," or "you ought to." As we hear another's comments, each of us is free to decide if those ideas resonate with our experience or not, accepting those ideas as helpful or setting them aside.

Another model for our group work is to stick mostly to "I statements." In other words, we can say things like, "I feel this way," or "I have experienced this in a similar

---

[19] Margaret Guenther, *Holy Listening: The Art of Spiritual Direction* (Cambridge, MA: Cowley Publications, 1992), 30, 19.

situation." We may *gently* offer our ideas on another person's meditational images and experiences, but always owning them as *our* projections or interpretations that may or may not resonate with the meditating person.

Silence is also an important part of our discussions together. God often needs our silence in order to speak to us. The other members of the circle may also need our silence in order to share with the group. Extroverts may begin talking several seconds sooner than more introverted folks. We may all need to wait a few uncomfortable moments before we jump in and talk. We may also need to limit how many times we speak up. If we find ourselves commenting after every person has shared his or her quiet time experience, it is time to refrain from speaking for a while. Studying the pattern on a rug, pillow, or picture is a good way to pass the waiting-in-silence time. Even if no one speaks up, we can say our closing prayer, go home, and know that God has still been working among us.

All our conversations must also be treated with *strict confidentiality* as we practice what author Margaret Guenther called "Holy Forgetting."[20] Everything that is said in this room stays in this room, with one exception. Sharing our own experiences with people outside the gathering is within the guidelines and may help a new person decide to come and try our group process for themselves. However, all the other members' words must stay in this room.

Using these guidelines can help us create an atmosphere of gentleness and trust, where we can safely bring up our sensitive, troubled, or joyful thoughts and experiences. Practicing this "assists" method and "Holy Forgetting," each one of us assists in the process of discerning where God may be leading us.

---

[20] Margaret Guenther, *Holy Listening: The Art of Spiritual Direction* (Cambridge, MA: Cowley Publications, 1992), 30, 19.

THE FAMOUS STATUE MEDITATION

Perhaps one of the most constant themes of our meditation in the group was how God accepted each of us just as we were. One evening, Pamela brought an exercise from the book *Sadhana* by Anthony de Mello. The author asks the reader to imagine that a sculptor has been commissioned to create a statue of himself or herself. The suggested scene is full of imaginative details. The reader enters a darkened room and sees the statue, walks around it, touches it, and registers his or her reaction to the statue. The reader speaks whatever he or she wants to the statue and then becomes that piece of sculpture. Jesus enters the room, sees the person-as-sculpture, and speaks to him or her. Jesus leaves the room, and the reader is asked to become herself or himself again, noticing any changes in feelings toward himself or herself.[21]

Three women of our group, Emily, Sharon, and Melinda, graphically remembered the meeting when the statue meditation was used (before I joined the group). They described their experiences to me for my seminary master's thesis. I'll let these wonderful women speak for themselves.

First, Emily, the choir member who interested me in attending the meetings, talked about that evening. "Oh yes, I remember the so-called statue meditation. (Laughs.) I don't know how Pamela approached it, but we were to imagine ourselves on a pedestal, naked, and I guess Jesus was supposed to be there. As I talked about it later in the meeting, I had to laugh because I was not naked in my meditation; I was in a choir robe!

---

[21] Anthony de Mello, *Sadhana. A Way to God: Christian Exercises in Eastern Form* (New York: Doubleday, 1984), 87–88.

"And I was in a choir robe not because I think I have a glorious voice and that personifies who I am. I was in a choir robe because I could not face my naked self, my naked *physical* self. I didn't want anyone to see my physical imperfections. I was more than embarrassed; I felt *guilty*, you know, as if I shouldn't have allowed this 'temple of my body' to become so defiled.

"It was laughable because I was expecting to hide my body from Jesus, who, I feel, knows my every thought. What good was it to be hiding in a choir robe? Obviously, the choir robe was so that *I wouldn't have to look at myself.*

"But the overall thing I experienced that night was *the affirmation, the gut knowledge* that *I am accepted by God just as I am.* That has helped me on my spiritual journey more than anything, because it has freed me to move from where I am.

"We spend so much time defending the fortress instead of letting down the drawbridge. But really feeling that love and acceptance allows you to take the steps you need to take day by day. Even though the people around you may still disapprove of you or what you're doing, you have the courage to continue because you have felt loved and affirmed. My experiences in our group of that acceptance by God freed me to have that courage."

Sharon, a librarian with a keen interest in art, was also at the meeting the night of the statue meditation. Here's what she said about her meditation. "One meditation that I can remember that was particularly outstanding had to do with achievement and what I was to do in my life. It just so happened that the meditation that night involved imaging yourself as a sculpture. I had not said anything to Pam about my intense art interest. This just happened to be what she was doing with us that night.

"She said to imagine yourself as a sculpture and imagine that Jesus is coming to look at you and imagine what Jesus is going to say. Well, as I was meditating on this, I pictured myself as a metal tree with leaves and flowers, made out of that verdigris-finish sculpture that has bits of gold and greenish-blue on it.

"When Jesus came to look at me, initially I was frightened, because I remembered the story of the fig tree that wasn't producing and how Jesus went and zapped it because he was so angry. I was very apprehensive about what Jesus would say or do when he approached me.

"To my surprise, Jesus walked up to me, walked around, looked at me, and said, 'Well done, thou good and loyal servant.'

"I had been flowering and leafing away as hard as I could because I knew Jesus was going to be looking. And the more Jesus praised me and praised what I was doing, the better I felt, and I relaxed and flowered even more!"

Melinda, our member with an earthy sense of humor, also spoke to me about that evening's meditation. "Ah, the famous statue meditation! This is what I wrote about that meditation":

> 'June 22, 1987. I am uncomfortable visualizing my physical self, myself as other, as idealized other, because this is a source of conflict. But in my meditation, I imagine that I go to my basement studio, and there on a marble base is a white marble statue, with a Greek face, nude, one foot stepping forward, arms down, palms open showing stigmata. The belly is fully pregnant. As I look around the back, I see that the statue's buttocks are flesh, with goose bumps and pimples. When I touch them on the statue, I feel the touch myself.
>
> 'The statue's fingers are now trailing a drapery behind. Now the ends of the long hair are real and are gold-tinted, as if a person had been in the sun a lot. The warm, golden hair texture of the statue contrasts with the cool smoothness of the marble. More parts of the body turn fleshy as I examine them, the marble separating off from the skin like the brown, chocolate bonnet on a Carvel ice cream cone. The pregnant belly is tan, with skin stretched tight over a lumpy fetus. At no time do I see the face.
>
> 'As I take the place of the statue, I feel the sadness in the stance, the downcast face, the trailing drapery. I

look out ahead of me, and the studio wall melts into a turquoise ocean with white foam and cool sand.

'Jesus enters the scene and looks around me, and then he encourages me to go into the water. I don't want Him beside me, being a lifeguard, or swimming with me. I want Him right behind me without me looking.'

Chuckling, Melinda turned to me. "That's safe! It's like me informing Jesus, 'I know you're there, but don't try to tell me to do anything. And I don't want you to be right with me!' That's good, that's good! I'm saying, 'Just keep your distance, Jesus!'" She laughed again. Reading from her journal, Melinda continued,

'As I walk into the deep sand, I am sinking. I'm comfortable, but I don't want to be there.

'We are in a leafy green tree house. I am tan and lean. I have eaten a passion fruit, and it has stained my lips red. I am naked. Jesus is wearing jeans and a blue and white-striped T-shirt. He says, *You can be beautiful; I'll be your lover. You can be beautiful. You can be yourself.* He says this over and over.

'He climbs down a ladder. I stay, lie on my back, and look at the leaves. I want him there, and I want him to go away. His eyes were magnified, brown and warm, but distant and critical, too. I had to convince myself that he was looking with love.'

Melinda concluded, "See, now I look back and see that my insight was way ahead of what I had the capacity for emotionally. Spiritually, these meditations were great because they really got us where we *were*. We could have sat there and spun out all kinds of good-sounding ideas. But this meditation was really *where I was*, emotionally and spiritually."

Experiencing God's all-accepting love was one of the first and most repeated outcomes of our meetings and meditations. Trusting those experiences took longer.

THE BOTTLE ON THE BEACH

"Imagine yourself on a beach, quite alone but feeling completely safe. There's enough sunshine for you to feel pleasantly warm but not overly hot. You hear the waves lapping on the shore, the calling of seagulls, and the soft murmur of the wind in the pines. You're walking at the water's edge, watching the foam roll onto the sand at the leading border of the waves. You can feel your bare feet sinking into the damp sand as you walk. You can almost taste and smell the salt tang in the air. As you amble along, you notice that something has washed up on the shore just a few feet in front of you. You realize it's a bottle, so you walk over to it and pick it up. Inside is a description, in words or pictures, of your heart's desire. What is that desire?"

This depiction is how I often lead people into a guided meditation on their deepest hopes. The idea of the beach and a gift washing up came to me from my memories of Anne Morrow Lindberg's *Gift from the Sea*.[22] I also use a bit of scripture as I guide this meditation, saying to the group, "Psalm 37, verse 4 says, 'Take delight in God, who shall give you your heart's desires.'[23] Often our deepest heart's desire is also God's deepest desire for us. Look at what's in your bottle, even if it is only question marks on a scrap of paper. Wonder about what your deepest desire might be. Now notice that someone is approaching you on the beach. It is some God-figure—perhaps a member of the Trinity—Father, Son or Holy Spirit. However, it could be a loved one, alive or passed on, or a person

---

[22] Anne Morrow Lindbergh, *Gift from the Sea* (NY: Pantheon, 1955).
[23] The Order of St. Helena, *The Saint Helena Psalter* (NY: Church Publishing Incorporated, 2004), 53.

from history or from scripture, or any representation of the Divine that comes to you. Speak with that God-figure about your heart's desire."

Duke entered this scene in meditation at a workshop I led at a spirituality conference. He shared with me and the group: "When you asked what was my heart's desire, my two grandchildren popped into my consciousness. A lot of times for me, the important thing in meditation is what pops into my conscious thought. I went with that image of my grandchildren. I thought to myself, *I might not have too much time left*, worrying that I might not be around for my two grandchildren much longer. My God-image was a bit unusual. God was a mist in front of me, but that image was quite satisfying. My mist said to me, 'Spend your remaining time with your grandchildren so that their memories of you will be a blessing to them when you are gone.' That was a wonderful answer."

I love using this "bottle on the beach" meditation because it can help conjure up wondrous images. Sometimes, however, this same envisioning scenario simply brings a person a feeling of peace or love, or results in an imaginary walk with Jesus, or an encounter with the Divine in a completely non-beach setting. I've come to believe that almost any story or topic will do for sparking meditation and envisioning. One person at a conference asked me which passages best help people use their imagination. I surprised myself by answering, "I don't think it matters what story I use. Almost any idea or passage seems to be effective because, ultimately, it is *God* who eagerly wants to communicate with us."

EMAIL ATTACHMENTS

On one memorable occasion, the modern technology of cellphones and emails produced striking imaginative results in meditation. I was speaking and listening over my cellphone with a man with whom I had worked in person as a spiritual director for more than a decade. We don't always meditate during phone sessions, but we had done so often enough that we were comfortable going into silence for about ten minutes near the end of that particular phone meeting. My directee was at a loss as to where God was calling him as a writer. An idea popped into my head, so after taking both of us through the relaxation process, I suggested that each of us read an imaginary email from God and open the various attachments that came with it.

After our silent period, Ted shared with me his meditative results. "The email message was quite clear," he told me. "God had written, 'Dear Ted, Haven't I always given you what you needed to do my work every time you needed it? Do you remember all the times I have provided exactly what was necessary at exactly the right time? I will do so again, now.' That reminder was very moving and reassuring. I did recall many times when what I needed was provided, almost miraculously, even when I seemed lost."

Moving on to the email attachments, Ted continued: "The first attachment was an image of a tree that had inspired me during a private retreat I took once, camping out in nature. I remember how I meditated on that tree's significance for me. These days, I'm aware of how trees are still moving me to write. The second attachment was a draft of the poem I wrote about that tree. The third attachment was a picture of a shelf of books by two of my favorite authors, with the message 'Read them.' I based my doctoral dissertation on these writers' works and want to craft a book on the social justice issues they address.

"The fourth attachment was a description of myself I'm not yet comfortable with—an identity I feel God is asking me to explore. It's a type of religious thinker or theologian, and I'm not sure exactly what that title means for me. In fact, I wanted to close that attachment rather quickly. The original email message and the first three attachments are calling me to trust, read, and to write—maybe about trees, maybe about social justice—but to continue to write. The last attachment means, I think, that God still wants me to wrestle with my identity as a *theological* author."

I was so struck by the vivid nature of Ted's meditation that I asked, and was given permission, to include his thoughts and images in this book. Imagining together over cellphones, over a distance of hundreds of miles, still seems a bit miraculous to me. However, I suppose it's no more amazing than envisioning with the Divine over the expanse of different dimensions. It all seems astonishing but, thankfully, quite real!

My own email attachments from God during that session seemed complete nonsense to me—a woman's name that might be a play on words, a 1950s jingle about margarine, and a name I've never heard of before. However, I've written everything down, to wait and see what meanings may come. Pondering over time is yet another wondrous way that shared imagination works, as I've detailed in the next chapter.

WHERE TO, MAC?

Sharing imagination over time is another branch of shared imagination that I've experienced, and it can happen in a variety of ways. Often, a woman ponders one of her own meditations and comes up with new insights as time goes by. In the spiritual direction group, our shepherdess, Pamela, would often suggest that we revisit a meditation by trying to reenter the thoughts or scenes at a later date. Ignatius, the inventor of this imagination-filled meditation process, also counseled "savoring" one's meditations over time.

Sarah, one of our group members, talked to me of the great value for her of allowing time for interpretations to surface so the depth of the meanings could fully develop. She explained, "I have dreams that are as much of a story as my meditations are, and I have learned to let myself sit with both the dreams and the meditations after writing them down. Sometimes it takes me years to interpret the symbolism. And if I rush that process, I crowd out, compress, and flatten the *richness* of the meaning that my imaginative life, and God, have cooked up for me."

Time has certainly helped bring out more meanings in one of my own meditations, which I titled "the taxicab driver." That meditative encounter came to me long ago, when my now-adult daughter was only one year old. That evening at the meeting, I saw myself in meditation as a passenger in an old-fashioned taxicab, where the wiper blades swung from the top of the windshield down, making upside-down half circles. The driver of the cab turned to me in the back seat and asked, almost in a Brooklyn accent, "Where to, Mac?"

A wave of longing washed over me as I replied, almost sobbing,

"Home!" Then, cartoonlike characters started smashing themselves on the windshield and were swept away by the old-fashioned wiper blades.

As I told the gathering my meditation, I remembered that my maiden name initials are MAC—Mary Ann Coe. I thought I was simply nostalgic for my home in Virginia and for my childhood life before the complications of marriage, children, and career in "big, bad New York City." I still think that was partly true.

But many years later, preparing to write my master's thesis, I thought about that meditation again. Suddenly, I realized that the taxicab scene could have been about my intense longing for a spiritual home, a longing that had found its answer precisely in my attending that spiritual direction gathering. I realized how that cabdriver could have been God asking me my heart's desire and that God was answering that deep desire by my being in the group. That cab was my safe space and transporter (the spiritual direction meetings). That cabdriver was God asking me what God already knew: I longed for a journey of self-discovery and God-discovery. And the old-fashioned wiper blades were the centuries-old process Ignatius developed to encourage imagination yet sweep away those things that are trivial and not heart-, God-, and love-centered.

What a wonderful image that cab has become for me! God is the driver, and God's cab was the safe transportation of the group and its method. Most emotionally for me, God was *asking me* where to go, illustrating the eternally *invitational* nature of the Divine One and the invitational nature of this imagination-filled process. I see the driver with great love now, inviting me, calling me by a name few people knew at that time. "Where to, MAC? Where would you like to go together, Mary Ann Coe? I will brush away the crazy, petty, annoying, and frightening distractions of your life. Where would you like to travel?" It is an image of God offering God's self as a confidant, a carrier to new places. But at the same time, the Holy One is always being invitational, not commanding or directive but asking, willing to go with, inviting. I have tears in my eyes as I see this God-figure today, tears of joy, and the same deep response: "Take me home, Lord, with you. For you are my home, in a land that sometimes seems frightening, cartoonlike, or petty. You are my home. I would go there. Be with me."

Why did it take a dozen years to understand the meaning of this meditation? I don't know. But maybe a bit of distance was necessary for me to comprehend this wonderfully detailed image of myself, God, and the imaginative meditation process.

TRUST AND RECURRING BASKETS

Imagining over time can bring trust in the process as well as an occasional recurring theme or image. Donna, who was in seminary to become a priest during my thesis-writing period, explained both gifts of time to me. "I think learning to *trust* the images that can come, or the insights that can occur in meditation was a really important education for me. Most of my meditation now, as then, tends to be in a prayer of quiet. Probably less than half of the time is it an interchange for me. It's more a matter of just resting in quiet, and then sometimes receiving images that come or little snippets of poetry or music."

Smiling, she went on, "But it was wonderful to be introduced to a space where imagery was okay, where it could be dealt with, and where, as strange as the imagery could be, it did not mean that I had gone off the deep end. I was reassured that, in that holy space and with discernment, possibly something holy was happening—in some way I was receiving gifts from God.

"For me," Donna continued, "the meditations that occurred over time, and reoccurred, and *continue to occur* are meditations with baskets. It was in this room that I started with basket meditations, and they continue to the present day."

Laughing, she said, "I guess the end result of the first two basket meditations was that I ended up in seminary! So, I guess they were significant. In the first meditation, I saw a basket, and I could draw it (and I did draw it later), and I could talk to God about it. But I wasn't allowed to open this basket. I took this image with me to a monastery on a retreat. I could actually feel the weight of it. I could describe its external components, but I wasn't allowed to open it in meditation.

Finally, one day in meditation, I was allowed to open it. That basket appeared as if it were a dollhouse but not a house that I knew. The second basket appeared in another meditation where God spoke to me, saying, 'You're not going to like this much. Pieces of this you're not going to like at all.' I thought to myself, *Oh great, let's get rid of this basket.* But when that basket came out, it was the facade of my own house here in town. It looked just the same, just like my house, with its stone wall. However, the entire back of the house had been knocked out. Whole new expansions of the house were being built, with odd-shaped rooms, and balconies on the second floor. The message seemed to be God saying, 'Your life is currently in the process of being remade, and while it may look the same on the outside, *go around to the back door!*'"

Donna went on to talk about a meditational basket that keeps showing up, but for which she has no interpretation yet. "Two summers ago," Donna told me, "while I was interning as a hospital chaplain, suddenly another basket showed up! It was a woven reed basket, probably thirty inches tall, big, and round. It was full of stuff and so heavy that I couldn't lift it. I wasn't even able to move it. In that meditation, other people came to help me empty the basket. I couldn't budge it, but others helped me empty that basket. That basket is still in my meditations, but it remains empty."

This engaging priest-in-training continued, "Then, last summer another basket appeared. It's a small basket that you can see through, as if the weaving is a type of filigree. I can see gold fabric lining it, and little bits of what looks like red velvet. I wasn't allowed to open that one either for a while. But once, on Christmas Eve, I was sitting very quietly at another church listening to music, when the musicians started to play Mozart's 'Ave Verum'! *Very appropriate Christmas music!* I thought. *It's an Easter piece!* However, I wasn't sure anyone else knew it was about the Crucifixion, and I guess I just zoned out during that part of the service. Then, suddenly, my filigree basket's lid came off. Inside was something that looked like a crown with a cross highly decorated with gems. It turned out to be a fancy doorknob cover! I laughed to myself, thinking, *Now what do I do with this?* Then God put that cover on a doorknob and opened the door. There I was in this beautiful valley! I was in this spacious, graceful, grace-filled place where I could just *be*. Since then,

I've realized that this doorknob cover is a gift from God to me, so that even when I end up in a place where they play Crucifixion music on Christmas Eve, I can go where there's graced space to be found. So, those are my baskets, and they show up from time to time. I'm curious to find out what will go in this lovely, big, serviceable basket that can carry quite a load but remains empty. I'm waiting to see if I might be told what ought to go in there."

The gift of time in this process also helped us women to let go of the fears, anxieties, and questions we may have brought with us as we joined the group. We began to actually enjoy being in a place where we could talk about our inner lives, our joys and troubles, and where we could listen for God speaking back to us through our imagination and through the other women of the group. Sharon, our artist, described to me her journey over time from apprehension and skepticism to trust. She began, "I remember I felt wary and reluctant to open up initially. This spiritual direction room *is a special place*, different from the world, but you don't know that it's safe right away. I brought all the assumptions from 'out there in the world'—the assumptions that you have to protect yourself, you have to be careful. I brought assumptions from work and from dealing with emotions in my family. All the many exchanges we have—legal, monetary—they all tell us it is not safe to be totally open. But in here, in this room, it is safe. Because this room is a safe place, people have felt free to open up here. It has been amazing to me, coming from the outside world where it's not always safe to bare our hearts, that nobody to my knowledge has taken advantage of the personal revelations that have occurred in this room."

Sharon went on, "I also remember that at first I felt a certain amount of skepticism about the process of the group. I recall thinking, *Is this silly? Is this unrealistic? The age of revelation is over, you know. Can it still happen here? Are people talking to themselves or letting their imaginations run away with them? Is this experience for real or not?* The first several sessions, I was skeptical, not knowing how to meditate, never having really tried before. I thought, *Can I do this? Am I going to have anything to say?* One thing that helped was reading John Sanford's books as I began coming to this group. The experience over time in the group reinforced the connection that he made between the collective unconscious and God.[24] (See this book's chapter "Similarities with Jung.") I asked Pamela once, 'Are these images just coming from my subconscious, or are they really images from God?' She had a wonderful answer to that. She said, 'They're both, because the subconscious is closer to God than the conscious mind.' So, between her saying that and my reading of John Sanford, I was able to put together that the subconscious can be a channel to God."

---

[24] John A. Sanford, *Dreams: God's Forgotten Language* (HarperSanFrancisco, 1968, 1989), 21, 31.

A THREEFOLD SHARING

There were times when three people were involved in sharing imagination over time. In the following story, one group member used another person's previous meditation to help a third individual (me) understand my own meditation that evening. It sounds complicated, but it's really not. Here's how that threefold sharing process happened to me.

At one of our meetings, I had been struggling in my meditation, asking God how I might feel more *individually* recognized in my professional music-making. It sounds pretty narcissistic to me now. However, at that time, I wanted more specifics in my meditation, and I wasn't getting them. I was a bit like a greedy child!

When I told the group about my struggle in meditation, Jill spoke up with just the right answer for that child. "I remember one night here, that Jean (Remember her? She moved away several years ago) had seen in her meditation this beautifully wrapped box, which Jesus had given her. But Jesus had told her she couldn't open it right now. So, Jean rested comfortably, just gazing at that beautiful box in her lap."

After hearing Jean's meditational image, I thought, *I want a box! I want to know that there is something wonderful waiting for me, even though I may not know exactly what it is yet.*

Turning to me, Jill suggested, "Mary Ann, maybe you need a box too. Maybe you would feel better knowing that something beautiful is coming, even though you don't know the details of it right now."

Suddenly, I rejoiced at the concept of a beautifully wrapped present from God waiting for me in my lap. I could *feel* that package in my future, even though I couldn't imagine the details. Seeing it as a lovingly wrapped, gorgeously decorated treasure from God suddenly made all the difference. I was no longer anxious about the details—I could simply rest in the knowledge that God had beautiful plans for me. What a gift that story was to me! And it came from a woman of the group, who remembered yet another woman's meditation from years before!

How I would have chafed at the time to be told to "wait on God!" But the tale of the box, simply and generously told from one woman through another woman, to me, was a beautiful gift of imagination and invited me to wait in a way that *telling* me to wait would never have worked for my impatient, child-before-Christmas-Day self.

The shared imagination process seems to get better with time. God works wonders helping us more fully understand a meditation as the years go by. And sometimes we women act as earthen vessels holding imaginative treasures, reminding each other of old but significant stories and images.

EXPLORING IMAGES AND USING DREAM METHODS

The way in which our group leader, Pamela, helped us search for meanings in our meditations involved reflection and intuition. Most often, she encouraged us to talk through our thoughts and images and search aloud for possible meanings. The other women of the circle would often make gentle comments or questions of their own, reflecting on what they felt specific images might mean. The woman describing her own meditation was encouraged to see if the ideas of the others resonated with her own feelings about the meditation.

Very often, a woman would come up with her own interpretation through this process. I remember a wonderfully crazy set of images that came to Donna one night, which none of us could make sense of but which Donna eventually figured out in a beautiful way.

Donna's meditation started with the image of an old-fashioned coffeemaker, the kind with the glass bubble on top, which Donna could remember from her childhood. In her meditation, Donna could see the coffee percolating up into that glass bubble, the water gradually becoming darker as the coffee brewed. Then she saw a fountain with water jetting out in all directions. Next came the image of a spider web, then lastly the image of a shattered mirror, with broken lines radiating out from the center.

Donna was encouraged to verbally investigate the details of each image, and after a while, she noticed that the fountain, the spider web, and the broken mirror all had lines emanating out from a central space. She connected that idea to her own life with this explanation. "I think all those images are about me, as I'm about to be ordained a priest. I think the lines mean how much one person's actions can reach out and affect others, the way that my new life as a priest can reach out and touch other people."

I remember being amazed at the wonderful connections Donna made between her seemingly disparate images. That's how the process worked. Most often, the meditating woman verbally figured things out for herself. And sometimes, we women in the circle helped in the interpreting. On that evening, I noticed that the old-fashioned coffee maker still hadn't been explained. It made me think about a connection between serving others and Donna's childhood. I voiced those ideas and asked if her desire to reach out and help others might have started in her childhood.

Donna smiled and replied, "Yes, many people are now telling me that they've always seen in me a desire to serve others. They say they're not surprised that I'm becoming a priest. I think I'm beginning to believe that I really am supposed to follow this path to ordination."

As I write today, I wonder if the percolating coffee in Donna's meditation could also have been about how the Spirit was percolating within her, culminating in her becoming a priest—like the coffee reaching full potency before being poured out for others.

Our process of interpreting meditations also seems very similar to some dream analysis methods. The imaginative, surprising things that come in both dreams and meditations are, I believe, a synthesis of one's imagination and the Divine. In fact, I've come to think of meditations as "waking dreams" and to value and utilize two specific dream-interpreting methods.

The first is a technique I learned about at a Haden Institute Dream Conference at the Kanuga Conference Center in North Carolina. One of the themes of that conference was that dreams come from the Divine in the service of "health and wholeness"[25]—for individuals, for groups, and even for the world. In the institute's dream interpretation system, after a person has related his or her dream, the other members of the

_____

[25] The Rev. Robert L. Haden Jr., *Unopened Letters from God: A Workbook for Individuals and Groups* (Haden Institute Publishing, 2010), 3.

small group start their comments with "In *my* dream," and then go on to describe what that nighttime vision might mean to them if they had been the dreamer.[26]

I think our group interpreting process is extremely similar to the Haden Institute "in my dream" method, even though we don't say, "in my meditation." Much like the workings of a dream group, in our spiritual direction circle, we are intuiting ourselves into another person's visionary experience. As in the dream gathering, our members then go on to gently speculate on what certain images or thoughts might mean to us if *we* had experienced them. And just as some people can use help interpreting dreams via the kind workings of a group, so too can meditations yield fruit when they go through the gentle talking across the circle process that Pamela invented in her group model.

Another dream interpretation process that has proved helpful to me is based on one of Gayle Delaney's methods, which begins with the dreamer describing in as much detail as possible each of the six parts of a dream: the setting, the people, the animals, the objects, the feelings, the actions. Once as much detail as possible has been mined, the dream interviewer asks a bridge question, such as, "Does _____, which you describe as _____ (restate the description once again), remind you of anything or anyone or of any part of yourself?" Delaney's process of using details and a bridge question to unpack the meaning in a dream has many well-crafted steps and is worth reading and studying.[27] I have found that meditations can share with dreams that emerging of surprising, almost unconscious details and can benefit from utilizing Delaney's dream method.

Sometimes in our meetings, however, the meditating woman was not ready to see the meaning of her own meditation. That's when we women learned some valuable lessons on silence. In fact, many aspects of silence became important as we in the circle experienced shared imagination. And, although *speaking* about *silence* seems to be a contradiction in terms, I'll explore that essential element in the following chapter.

---

[26] Haden Institute Summer Dream Conference lectures, 2008.

[27] Gayle Delaney, PhD, *The Dream Kit: An All-in-One Toolkit for Understanding Your Dreams* (HarperSanFrancisco, 1995), 11–25.

THE VALUE OF SILENCE

Over time, silence became a treasured and trusted element of our spiritual direction meetings, but it was not always so. Most of us in the group were not used to being in silence for any length of time, but with Pamela's help, we learned to value quietness at different points of the meetings and for different reasons.

Pamela would, on occasion, ask us to enter the meeting room in silence. At other times, she would suggest that we begin the gathering by each of us "checking in"—going around the circle having each woman describe briefly how she felt that night or what was going on in her life at that moment. Silence was important in both types of beginnings. Entering the room in silence dramatically set that time apart from everyday life. Listening silently to each other's "checking in" tuned us into listening to the Divine in meditation and to each other in the discussion period after meditation.

We also became accustomed to the lengthening period of silence during which Pamela allowed us to meditate. Emily later told me, "At first, five minutes seemed so *long* to meditate, but as we did it more often, we got used to the lengthening time, and sometimes twenty minutes or more would go by, and we barely noticed."

Sarah, our young opera singer, valued the shared silence immensely. She explained to me, "I would say that probably the most powerful gift to me of those meetings was *the shared silence*. It was the experience of feeling the presence, even hearing the breathing of the other women in this room all being in silence communally. We were all making a commitment, not just to show up to that door but to the *silence together*. How many other experiences do we have of intentionally created silence in community? It felt very intentional. We were all *listening together,* which has a power that has a qualitative difference, I think, from listening alone. That spiritual listening together is something that group provided for me that I have had no other experience of."

Additionally, we learned to allow some silence right after the meditation time. Pamela would ask, "How did that go for any of you?" She would then stare at the pattern in the room's rug, patiently waiting to see if a person would speak up. Silence was okay, Pamela would always tell us. If no one shared that evening, we would simply say our close-of-day prayers and go home, knowing that God had been at work in our midst even without any discussion.

Pamela also asked us to wait a bit after a woman's comments before jumping in with a thought of our own. She explained that more introverted people may need time before they speak up. Pamela asked us all to wait longer than might be comfortable, in order to let others speak first.

I remember how hard it was for me to be silent when I thought I knew "the answer" for some woman about her meditation or life, especially when it seemed as if that woman was just not getting it! At one meeting, I tried all sorts of leading questions with someone in the group who just couldn't see what her meditation was pointing to (according to me!). Pamela spoke with me privately later and agreed with my interpretation but stressed that each woman had to come to her own interpretation *in her own time.* Sometimes the difficult truth is staring us in the face, but we can't or won't see it. Our shepherdess taught me that trying to make someone face a painful reality usually is not successful and is too forceful for spiritual work.

On a lighter note, another group member, Melinda, also had trouble keeping silent at times during the meeting, but her descriptions of herself are quite funny. I'll let her explain her general learning process (to keep quiet) and a pointedly funny message from God during one of her meditations.

Melinda launched her tale: "I remember being in a meditation and feeling all worked up. Some issue had been going on for a number of weeks with some people in the group, I don't remember who. But the answer to their problem seemed perfectly obvious to me, even though *they* didn't seem to see it. I felt like they were just stupid, and I just had to set them straight. So, I was asking God, 'What do you want me to say? What do you want me to say? Just tell me the words. I don't know how to make it right, and I so much want to make it right. Just tell me, God, what am I supposed to say?' I got a direct answer that really startled me.

"'Just listen.'

"And I was stunned. You know that it's God when it's not what you thought you wanted to hear. I expected to be given some *words to say*. It really had that feeling of somebody speaking to me, somebody answering me. That was really a moment of stunning clarity. I thought, *You sure, God? You sure I'm supposed to just listen?* The answer was completely convincing. There was no question that 'just listen' was what I was supposed to do."

With her infectious laughter, this delightful woman continued, "There *was* a question about whether I *could* just listen or whether I *wanted* to!" Melinda chuckled again. "But there was no question that I was being given a direction. And the fruits of that meditation are that I've never restrained myself and regretted it. So far so good on that one! Ha-ha! I'll let you know if I'm ever listening *too much*." More belly laughs erupted from this earthy and spiritual woman!

During this formative time when we women began in the spiritual direction group, we learned how being silent is essential for meditation, the value of shared silence, the need for silence to allow others to speak, and the imperative to never tell another group member what she should believe or understand. And yes, I personally learned some lessons on the opposite of silence: when to speak—as I began to practice being a spiritual director.

WHEN TO SPEAK, WITH DISCLAIMERS

In seminary, we learned by doing. In that spirit, one time I was assigned to another female student in a process called dyads. Basically, in dyads, two students would go to a quiet spot together, and for the first half hour, one would be the director (to listen and guide), and one would be the directee (to talk about his or her life). We would then switch roles for the next half hour.

As the director, listening to my dyad partner describing her marriage, a really strong intuitive feeling popped into my head. The idea seemed much too personal and too presumptuous for me to say to her. So, I kept silent. However, the idea banged so loudly inside my head I finally did speak my thought, with lots of disclaimers: that I might be wrong, that she would need to see if my idea resonated with her, and so on. I was prepared for her to be offended by my seemingly too personal idea, but she was amazed and grateful. She couldn't believe that I had hit the mark so well regarding this difficulty she was describing.

She wasn't the only one who was amazed. I couldn't believe I was supposed to say what had popped into my head! That experience and other similar ones over time led me to begin to trust the ideas that came to me as I listened intuitively in spiritual direction. I learned that if an idea would simply not leave my mind, if it kept banging around inside my brain, then I needed to say it.

I tried that idea out at the very first meeting when I officially took over as the leader of Pamela's group, after she had moved away. In the discussion period after the meditation, I remember tentatively saying to each woman the ideas that came to me and wouldn't leave my mind. Amazingly, each idea seemed to resonate with that woman, or seemed to touch her deeply, or to open up another viewpoint for her. It was a heartwarming, slightly heady experience. I felt as if I were becoming my name—Archer—shooting spiritual arrows into people's hearts.

Don't misunderstand me. I'm certainly not always right, and I *always* give many disclaimers before I speak, counseling that I might be wrong or that my ideas might not resonate with or be helpful for that person.

In fact, one of my most lovable spiritual directees expressed to me that I deliver too many disclaimers, telling me, "Mary Ann, just say it. Whatever it is usually is very instructive."

For me, it's a matter of waiting long enough to see if the idea keeps banging against the inside of my skull. If something won't stop hounding me, I speak the thought, with lots of cautionary statements.

On the other hand, there are plenty of times when I don't have any idea come to me as a person is speaking in spiritual direction. That's when being silent can seem really awkward. Sometimes I panic and think, *I'm the professional here. I'm supposed to think of something wise to say, and I can't think of a single thing.*

However, I've learned that when nothing comes, say nothing. The process of listening as a director or shepherdess is one of intuitively hearing a person's story while being open imaginatively to divine ideas that spring up. For me, when no idea comes, I simply must stay silent and keep listening. But when a thought won't go away, I need to speak it. It's a delicate balancing act, but it is so rewarding when the directee and I find new ideas or directions from God for that person's journey at the right moment.

Each director in one-on-one spiritual direction and each member of a spiritual direction group will have different methods and say different things, but that's the beauty of shared imagination. God can only work through each specific, flawed-but-real individual and each person's mind, intuition, and imagination.

TESTING MEDITATIONAL INSIGHTS

God can and does speak to our hearts, minds, intuition, feelings, and creativity. Sometimes the hardest thing for us to learn is to trust that inner voice. How can we know if the thoughts and ideas that come are from God?

Pamela always counseled us to "test the fruits" of our meditations over time, to see if the ideas and inspirations that came in our quiet time led our thoughts, feelings, and actions *toward* God/Love or *away from* God/Love. How have our "inspirations" shaped our emotions and our dealings with ourselves, others, and God?

Melinda spoke to me about this turning to God, and perhaps because she is an artist, she used a visual example of a plant turning toward the light. "Well, I feel like the journey toward God follows a sort of similar path in many people. First, there's the period of your life before the journey, where you may be searching or making attempts to look for the right thing, the thing that's going to satisfy you. And then there's the time when you recognize what it is that you actually need to be oriented toward. You sort of see that there's a light. You realize that toward the light is where you're supposed to go and that there's no turning back to the other way. And then there's the process of growing toward the light. It's sort of like the plant that has found where the sun is, and the rest of its energy is oriented toward being pointed in that direction and getting nourishment from that source. Even if circumstances happen that sort of push you in the wrong direction, you kind of keep turning back. Heliotropism it's called in plants."

Testing the fruits also involves looking within ourselves for the qualities that Paul lists in Galatians 5:22, "The fruit of the Spirit is love, joy, peace, patience, kindness, generosity, faithfulness, gentleness, and self-control."[28]

There is a beautiful Moravian hymn by Johann Christian Geisler titled "The Fruit of the Spirit," which lists those qualities with slightly different and even more lovely words: "The fruit of the Spirit is Love, Joy, Peace, Patience, Friendliness, Gentleness, Faith, Hope, Truth, and Kindness."[29] Once, when I was extremely angry with someone, the gentle, repetitive tune of that hymn kept running through my mind all one night and into the next morning. At first, I thought I was hearing that music because I had just played flute on that choir piece in church. But when the melody would not leave my head, I finally realized that God was counseling me to turn toward those qualities. I rushed to find the sheet music to remind myself of those attributes and spoke in my mind the following prayer: "Thank you, Holy Spirit, for not giving up on me, for playing that song over and over again in my head until I would learn its words and try to live them. Help me keep trying to practice those fruits, one day at a time. I'm a stubborn, slow learner, but thanks for persisting with me. And help me remember, to embody, and to give flesh to those words through my own body, actions, and life."

Using two of my favorite prayers from author Anne Lamott, I ended with, "Help me, help me, help me. Thank you, thank you, thank you."[30]

Ignatius explained another helpful process, "testing the spirits" in meditation, differentiating by whether a person is turned *toward* or *away* from God. For those individuals who are actively turned away from the Holy One, the thoughts to distrust in contemplation are ones that counsel increased pleasures and gratification. The trustworthy ideas are remorse and the sting of one's conscience. For people who are trying to live as God would lead them, the concepts to believe in are courage, strength, consolation, hope, tears of joy, inspiration, and peace. Harsh,

---

[28] Bruce M. Metzger and Roland E. Murphy, eds., *The New Oxford Annotated Bible, New Revised Standard Version* (NY: Oxford University Press, 1991), 270 NT.

[29] Johann Christian Geisler, *The Fruit of the Spirit* (Salem, NC: Moravian Music Foundation, 2012).

[30] Anne Lamott, *Help Thanks Wow: The Three Essential Prayers* (NY: Penguin Group, 2012), 15.

critical thoughts in meditation, along with the sadness of seemingly insurmountable obstacles, are not to be trusted.[31]

Carla, a member of a summer group I formed in the upper Midwest, experienced really troubling thoughts in one meditation, which prompted me to explain Ignatius's discernment of spirits—to the benefit of all the women present that night.

Carla remembered out loud to me, "I think back to that 'evil presence meditation' I had. I was sitting there in our meeting circle and hearing Jesus say something to me like, 'Well, you're doing this wrong!' Or he was saying, 'Well, you just think you're too important.' I was *miserable*. I had to leave the room and went sobbing to the bathroom. When I came back to the group and shared my meditation, you talked about St. Ignatius and his discernment of spirits. Now I know to ask, 'Is this you, Jesus?' Ha, Ha! It's as simple as telling myself, 'Now, wait a second. My man Jesus does *not* talk to me that way!' He may provide for me moments of humility to work through, but there's no way that my Savior is telling me I'm not good enough or that I'm expecting too much. No way is *He* dismantling my self-esteem.

"That meditation was *powerful*. It was in-my-body powerful! I can hardly explain how bad I felt as I was sitting there in meditation. I felt agitated and awful enough to get up and leave our meeting room. It was overpowering for me because, although I cry at lots of different times, it wasn't like that. It felt like …" Carla pauses. "You're going to laugh, but you've read the Harry Potter books, right?"

"Oh yes," I quickly replied, "I'm a huge Harry Potter fan."

"Well, it felt like the *dementors*[32] were attacking me! I imagined that feeling of 'nothing is going to be good again.' It was really that overwhelming. I was grateful for what I took away from that meditation and meeting—I need to ask the question, 'Is this you, Jesus?' I need to be aware that if my thoughts are taking me in a direction that is dismantling the good that I am, then something wrong and funky is going on here, and it's probably not from God."

---

[31] Thomas Corbishley, SJ, translator, *The Spiritual Exercises of Saint Ignatius* (Wheathampstead, Hertfordshire, England: Anthony Clarke Books, 1973), 107.

[32] J. K. Rowling, *Harry Potter and the Prisoner of Azkaban* (NY: Scholastic Press, 1999), 85.

I said, "I think it was helpful for the whole group, too, because I had never explained the discernment of spirits, maybe because disturbing meditations came up so seldom in that meeting format. However, the women in our circle needed to know that when negative, harsh, judgmental ideas or images happen in meditation, those are not from God."

"Exactly," Carla affirmed. "I remember that book, *Good Goats, Healing Our Image of God*, which you brought in. One of the first pages described the author's childhood image of a domineering, punishing God.[33] Well, many of us grew up with that image. I think our spiritual direction gatherings were a place of healing those God-images for me. I became able to say, 'No. It doesn't work that way. God is not a punisher.'

"I'm really confident of that truth, even to this day. The punishing image was the false God I was hearing in my head in that disturbing meditation, and clearly something inside me knew it was not right. So now I have tools—St. Ignatius's wisdom that you passed on that night. Now I know to say to myself, 'This doesn't seem right. This cannot be from God.'"

I agree with Carla! I believe that the women who have attended these spiritual direction meetings fall into Ignatius's second category—those who are trying to live in tune with God's intentions. I think of us as sunflowers, continually trying to turn toward the light of God. Whenever disturbing, harsh, judgmental, or fearful images surfaced in our meditations—usually extremely rarely—Pamela always advised us to call on God for protection, to ask ourselves if what we saw or heard was in line with a loving God, and to look squarely at those images again to see if they changed into something less frightening. Confronted by anything at all frightening in meditation, I usually ask, "Is this really you, Jesus?" In my experience, the disturbing thoughts have no answer and simply flee. Even in meditations where God seems to offer us corrections of our actions or beliefs, these necessary changes are suggested quite simply (though sometimes firmly) but without harshness or judgmental qualities. Fearful, negative, condemning elements in a contemplation are probably not from God, while insights that bring joy,

---

[33] Dennis Linn, Sheila Fabricant Linn, and Matthew Linn, *Good Goats: Healing Our Image of God* (Mahwah, NJ: Paulist Press, 1994), 3.

peacefulness, consolation, and deep tears of feeling acceptable to the Holy One are very likely from the Divine. I often back up my assessment with the words from Psalm 37:4–7:

> Take delight in the Lord,
> and he shall give you your heart's desire.
> Commit your way to the Lord and put your trust in him,
> and he will bring it to pass.
> He will make your righteousness as clear as the light
> and your just dealing as the noonday.
> Be still before the Lord
> and wait patiently for him.[34]

Our heart's desire is often what comes in meditations, and that desire is usually from the Divine as we seek more and more to turn toward God, to trust and take delight in the Holy One.

Checking with trusted spiritual friends is also important in the shared imagination process. In the group meetings, we women accomplished this by sharing and listening to each other and to the leader. One can also consult with a spiritual director, or belong to a peer supervision group, or simply confide in a trusted friend, teacher, or clergy person.

Pamela told me of a new insight she gained from sharing a meditation with one of her professors at General Seminary. "I spoke to this woman professor about my meditation where I saw myself in a Fiat. I couldn't figure out what that car might mean, but my professor explained that cars sometimes symbolize life's journey. She also told me that 'fiat' in Latin means 'let it be done.' She suggested that I might be echoing in my own life Mary's willingness to be God's instrument when she answered the angel announcing Jesus's birth, 'Let it be according to Thy will.' I would never have thought of those ideas without telling that meditation to my professor!"

Sharing with others can also allow people to confide similar spiritual experiences to us. I read to my writing class about hearing in meditation

---

[34] *The Book of Common Prayer, according to the use of The Episcopal Church* (The Church Hymnal Corporation and Seabury Press, 1977), 633

a description of heaven from my baby girl who had miscarried when I was five months pregnant. After class, another woman in the group privately confided in me a similar experience of hearing about heaven from a daughter who had died. We have since become close spiritual friends.

Testing the ideas and spirits that come in meditation, along with confiding in trustworthy others can help us believe in our own spiritual experiences. It can help us feel a connection with others, keep us from self-delusion, and even bring us new insights.

SIMILARITIES WITH JUNG

There are some interesting similarities between my idea of shared imagination and several of Jung's concepts, especially his notions of the collective unconscious, active imagination, and synchronicity. Carl Jung (1875–1961) was a Swiss psychiatrist and psychoanalyst who founded analytical psychology. His work greatly influenced not only the field of psychiatry but also anthropology, archaeology, literature, philosophy, and religious studies. According to Sonu Shamdasani, the editor of Jung's *The Red Book*, Jung's "childhood dreams, visions, and fantasies" helped propel Jung into his vocation.[35] As a boy of twelve, Jung experienced a vision of God unleashing a huge turd on the cathedral in Basel, an experience that came with a sense of bliss and release. He felt this image was a direct experience of God, who was all-powerful but who was free of and above the Bible and the church. That imaginative event, coupled with his lack of any feeling on the day of his First Communion, led him to abandon organized Christianity.[36] However, Jung continued throughout his life to be interested in spiritualism,[37] mythology,[38] and in God.

Some people to whom I've described my shared imagination concept have found in its process a connection to Jung's idea of the

---

[35] C.G. Jung, *The Red Book: Liber Novus, A Reader's Edition*, Sonu Shamdasani editor (NY: W.W. Norton & Company, 2009), 4.

[36] Ibid., 5.

[37] Ibid., 6–7.

[38] Ibid., 12.

collective unconscious.[39] Jung theorized that there are two layers of the unconscious in an individual. The first layer is the personal unconscious and consists of ideas acquired during one's lifetime. The second layer he called the collective unconscious and is inherited by being human.[40] Jung solidified his idea of the collective unconscious when World War I began. Shortly before combat commenced, Jung's repeated, disturbing visions of destruction made him fear he was going mad. The outbreak of the war convinced Jung that he was not going mad but that he had tapped into foreknowledge of the impending conflict via the collective unconscious.[41] In shared imagination, I believe one can connect with God, but those without a religious inclination or with a more psychological bent might call it a connection to Jung's idea of the collective unconscious or of his concept of Self (one's best self—the goal of individual human development).

Jung also coined the term "active imagination" and used various methods of this concept to work therapeutically with his patients.[42] He would induce waking fantasies in his patients by systematically eliminating critical attention and focusing on a mood. Symbolic visions of that mood would appear to his patients who could then paint, sculpt, or draw these symbols. Visual people would see images, audio-verbal types might hear words, some patients held dialogues between "the other voice" and themselves, and some experienced automatic writing. Understanding what came in these fantasies, with the help of the therapist, produced a therapeutic effect. The idea that words or images come to the imagining person to bring growth and wholeness is common to both my concept of shared imagination and Jung's active imagination. Also strikingly similar to me between active Jung's active imagination and my shared imagination are the various types of envisioning that occur in both methods—images, scenes, dialogues, imaginative letter-writing (see "Conversations, Dreams, and Letters" in this book), and receiving creative works (see "Poetry, Prose, and Music" also later in this

---

[39] C.G. Jung, *The Red Book: Liber Novus, A Reader's Edition*, Sonu Shamdasani editor (NY: W.W. Norton & Company, 2009), 50.
[40] Ibid.
[41] Ibid., 28.
[42] Ibid., 52.

work). I've come to believe that the process I call shared imagination is extremely close to Jung's idea of active imagination—with my own overlay of religious faith.

Jung practiced most deeply on this type of fantasy using *himself* as the subject. *The Red Book* was his journal of nightly inducing fantasies in himself—entering that fantasy world as an unfolding drama and writing down what came to him. The fruit of those years of imagining and studying was, according to Shamdasani, "Jung regains his soul and overcomes the contemporary malaise of spiritual alienation. This is ultimately achieved through enabling the rebirth of a new image of God in his soul and developing a new worldview in the form of a psychological and theological cosmology."[43]

I am amazed at Jung's courage to explore his own depth and that of the collective unconscious *by himself.* There were times when troubling images and conversations came to him, and he had to grip the edges of his table to keep some control and composure. Often he would have to bring himself out of these emotions by means of yoga practices.[44]

In our women's meetings, I trust that our fantasies will not dip into dangerous, disturbing worlds because the gatherings are grounded in God—by the relaxation process where we all breathe in God three times and by ending with the Compline prayer service. I've also written in a previous chapter, "Testing Meditative Insights," about ways to dispel negative, frightening thoughts or images that can come (albeit very infrequently in my own groups) during meditation.

Another similarity I've discovered between the real-life outcomes of shared imagination and Jung's ideas is something he called "synchronicities," events that he felt were connected by meaning rather than by cause.[45] For Jung, these occurrences did not cause each other, but they were somehow connected by the meaning they had for the individual. When I attended seminary, the phrase "God-incident" was often used to mean a spiritually laden happenstance that seemed to

---

[43] C.G. Jung, *The Red Book: Liber Novus, A Reader's Edition*, Sonu Shamdasani editor (NY: W.W. Norton & Company, 2009), 48.

[44] C.G. Jung, *The Red Book: Liber Novus, A Reader's Edition*, Sonu Shamdasani editor (NY: W.W. Norton & Company, 2009), 38.

[45] Richard Tarnas, *Cosmos and Psyche* (New York: Penguin Group, 2006), 50.

have a loving God behind the events. Nonreligious types may call such occurrences coincidences. In seminary, with the eyes of faith, we often sensed the Divine working behind the scene. Synchronicities and God-incidences are not identical, but they are events that can be connected by the *meaning* one puts on the occurrences. Interestingly, both types of events seem to happen more frequently the more one pays attention or becomes open to their possibility and reality.

I've come to the study of Jung's ideas rather late in life, but I must confess that I see many similarities between his concepts of the collective unconscious, the Self, active imagination, and synchronicities with my own experiences of shared imagination and its outcomes. It's really rather wonderful, and I look forward to learning even more about sharing with Jung!

GREEN APPLES

On one memorable occasion in a one-to-one meditative session, God gently reminded me of the nondirective role of a spiritual director as *listener* and not *lecturer*. That Godly correction was made sweeter by two surprising words: "green apples."

I was listening in a spiritual direction session to a man with whom I'd been working for over twelve years, when this person asked if he could stop talking for a while. I suggested we meditate in silence for a few moments, and I took both of us on the usual "relax-from-your-toes-up" talk. We pictured ourselves breathing in God's light, love, and healing power while handing over burdens. I then proposed that we speak in imagination to the Holy One about our present-day joys and sorrows.

During the first part of the quiet moments, I conversed in my mind and heart with the Divine about my own blessings and troubles. The real surprises came when I turned my attention to my directee. "What about this man's problems?" I asked in meditation. "What can I tell him from you, God?"

God immediately answered, without rancor, "You don't need to know anything at this moment. I am speaking with him quite directly right now."

Ouch! I thought and mentally stepped back, understanding that I was unnecessary in this equation. But I still wondered, like a greedy child, if I couldn't receive just a tidbit of insight. "Couldn't I get just a small idea to speak about with this man?" I questioned.

Like a patient parent, the Holy One relented and said, "Green. Green apples."

Confused, I remained silent.

God continued, "Green apples can be quite sour, like the sorrows in life. But you don't have to eat them raw. They are good for cooking, and they taste much better with great amounts of sugar, then baked between two delicious pie crusts. Sorrows, just like green apples, are better when you add the sugar and pie crust of prayer, sharing, and listening."

I was amazed and grateful for the metaphor of a green apple baked pie.

A few moments later, when I invited my directee to finish his own meditation and become present in the room again, he told me of astoundingly powerful words he seemed to hear directly from the Divine during the silence. I can't share those words, but I can say that both of us were moved to tears by the power of that holy communication about sorrow and pain.

As the session ended, I told my spiritual friend about the answers that came to me in meditation. We had a good laugh about my conversation, about God correcting my know-it-all desire yet relenting with a beautiful, unexpected image. I was reminded of Julian of Norwich's visions of the Divine being "as close to us as our clothing,"[46] "our courteous lord,"[47] and even as "our mother."[48] The Holy One certainly spoke directly to my friend in meditation that day, even while telling me in loving ways that I didn't need to be the source of all insight. But "our courteous lord" also answered my request for a slice of wisdom, giving me a cooking example of green apples made sweeter.

---

[46] Julian of Norwich, *Showings*, translated by Edmund Colledge, OSA, and James Walsh, SJ (NY: Paulist Press, 1978), 130.

[47] Ibid., 246.

[48] Ibid., 294.

GOOD SHEPHERDING QUALITIES

Pamela Barnett, our group's founder and original shepherdess, had much to say about the qualities of a good leader in a shared imagination group. She told me her thoughts as I was collecting stories for my master's thesis.

Pamela began, "In group spiritual direction, the leader does lead but with tones of *spiritual friendship*, more so than in one-to-one direction. The hierarchy, or power, or authority, of a *one-to-one* direction relationship is diluted in a *group* setting. Members of a group can also act as spiritual directors, though to a lesser extent than the leader."

She continued, "In group spiritual direction, the waters can become more muddied over boundary issues between friendship and authority, especially in a parish setting. The director needs to be aware of her own weaknesses and needs, her desire for power, for authority, for flattery, etcetera, in order to keep things as clear as possible. She needs to be able to catch things early if something is going off-track in the group discussion. Having one's own spiritual director and peer groups and colleagues helps a leader with self-examination as well as examination of the group's discussion practices.

"In guiding the discussions," Pamela further explained, "the leader needs to ask open-ended questions to help clarify an issue and to help the woman come to her own understanding of her life experience or meditation. Margaret Guenther provides examples of clarifying questions like, 'Could you say a little more about that?' 'Can you give me an example of what you mean by …?' 'Help me understand what you are saying.' 'Do you mean …?'[49] I also found it helpful to ask a woman, 'How does that feel to you?' 'Does that interpretation resonate with how you're feeling?'"

Pamela went on to explain to me what steps might need to be taken in the rare event that a single member becomes disruptive for the entire group. "Occasionally, there may be a member of the group whose presence and actions are actually destructive to the whole. Only once in my thirteen years as leader did this actually happen. A disruptive member of the group needs to be spoken with individually, outside the group setting. If that person continues to be disruptive, the spiritual director needs to speak with the priest in charge at her church to apprise him or her of the situation. The director/leader also needs to speak with her own therapist and spiritual director and spend time in prayer trying to discern what to do in this situation.

"It may be determined that the disruptive person needs to leave the group or else the group will disband of its own accord because the other members feel threatened and unsafe. Then the group leader needs to privately ask that person to leave and offer that member individual spiritual direction with another director or suggest the person seek professional therapy. The leader needs to tell the disruptive member that she may speak to their priest about the leader's decision to remove her from the group. As the leader, make sure your priest already knows about this situation and agrees with the actions you are taking."

Clasping her hands gently in front of her, Pamela summed up, "It is a very delicate operation, removing a member from a group. The director needs to look at herself to see if her own expectations, patterns, hot buttons, etcetera are setting off the situation. Also, at some point, the leader may need to inform the group of the impending removal of the disruptive member, when that person is not at a meeting. The other members may have important insights about the situation, but they are not responsible for the final decision."

Margaret Guenther, whose book *Holy Listening* inspired me to become a spiritual director, wrote the following insightful description

---

[49] Margaret Guenther, *Holy Listening: The Art of Spiritual Direction* (Boston, MA: Cowley Publications), 65.

of a spiritual director, a description that also fits the role of leader in a shared imagination group.

> The spiritual director is a midwife of the soul, present and attentive as new life emerges. The spiritual director offers hospitality, in the holy tradition of Abraham entertaining the angels. The spiritual director is a teacher, a rabbi, after the model of Jesus, who was called "Teacher" by those who loved him. But whether we call him teacher, midwife, or host, the spiritual director is always and above all a holy listener.
>
> The holy listener does not engage in friendly chats or problem-solving sessions. Rather, the conversation of spiritual direction occurs in the presence of God. As the twelfth-century Cistercian spiritual director Aelred of Rievaux said, "Here we are, you and I, and I hope a third, Christ Jesus, is in our midst." The holy listener knows that the space between himself and the directee is sacred space, God-filled space. And he knows that he does not work alone.
>
> So the spiritual director is able to put herself out of the way and thereby to be totally present to the person sitting opposite. Because she is disinterested (not at all the same as uninterested), she is able to listen critically but without judgment. She is able to ask hard questions, to sit comfortably with silence, not to be frightened by tears, and to rejoice in God's love. She is ready for whatever may come and immune to the temptation to "fix" anything. Above all, the spiritual director is humble and reverent, aware that she is being entrusted with another's very being.[50]

---

[50] Margaret Guenther, *The Practice of Prayer* (Boston, MA: Cowley Publications, 1998), 94–95.

REMEMBRANCES OF PAMELA

I'd like to share a few more snapshots of the qualities of our wise leader, Pamela, characteristics that are not absolutely necessary in a good shepherdess but that were endearing in this particular spiritual leader. I hope you enjoy as much as I do these stories of holy women in tiaras, a person with a musical overtone of self-doubt, and a patient listener to a "fizzy-bottle woman."

Sarah, our opera singer, spoke to me about qualities Pamela possessed that made her seem comforting, humble, and holy—almost like the medieval mystical women Sarah had studied so much in college. "I remember Pam as shepherdess," Sarah told me. "I remember the quality of her voice, the way that it was connected to the bottom of her gut very easily and naturally, and how low and deep her tone was. It was very grounding in meditation to hear this voice that was low, and soft, and very earthy.

"I also remember her jewelry," Sarah continued, "the holy way she wore it. That was another thing about Pam that I admired. I felt like the way she dressed and the way she wore her jewelry was like *holy adornment*—a quality that I longed for in myself."

Sarah explained, "It reminds me of a big controversy with the visionary nun Hildegard of Bingen (1098–1179), when someone was miffed with her and her monastic community because they were all wearing jewels and tiaras. Someone felt they had to step in and say that contemplative life should be about *simplicity*. Hildegard came right back and said something like 'We are brides of Christ, and we are adorning ourselves for the most lovely bridegroom we can imagine. This is one of the ways in which we offer ourselves to him.'"

Giggling, Sarah went on, "Just thinking of all these rich ladies with their dowries walking around, praying, and sitting in chapel with their tiaras on, it's kind of nice. Pam didn't strike me *quite* that way, but it always felt like she was adorning herself in a holy way, that she was conscious of a beautiful object put on her finger or around her wrist. She seemed like a holy woman to me, which seemed like a good person to be shepherding a group."

Borrowing from her experience as a musician, Sarah added, "I was continually struck by her interjection of self-doubt and self-criticism, if you could call it that, throughout the process of leading. It wasn't a loud, long, or a sour note; it was just like an *overtone* (inaudible high pitches that give a unique *color* to each instrumental or vocal note). Every now and then, Pamela would say, 'I don't really know if I'm doing this well, but this is what I think.' Again, it reminded me of the medieval mystic tradition, that one always made apology for one's transmission of God, because we are fallible human instruments, and we might not quite get it right. There might be something in us that is clouding the clear water that is coming through us. Pam's disclaimers reminded me of those medieval wise women."

Pamela also had the wonderful ability to make everyone feel *listened to* at each meeting, even when a woman might need more time to speak on a given night. At times in meetings, I talked more than my share of the discussion period because I was shaken up by life events. I coined the phrase "fizzy-bottle woman" to describe how I resembled a bottle of carbonated drink that had been shaken too hard and was about to overflow. At those times, I worried aloud to the group that I was taking up more than my share of the group discussion. Pamela would put me at ease, saying that I probably needed the extra time that night. She and the rest of the gathering simply concentrated on my words, listening intently, giving their own insights, asking thoughtful questions, and always giving generously of this special discussion time. To me, their generosity felt much like God's grace, God's sufficiency, God's giving us what we need when we need it.

Sarah, too, would sometimes feel like this fizzy-bottle woman. She experienced the freedom of being not only allowed but encouraged to talk more than the other women on a particular night. She explained it to me this way, "I love how Pamela and the group really listened to each other. I always had so much to say. What a strange, unusual thing for me!" Laughing, she went on, "I did feel at times like I had to somehow create a little corral for my horse to run around in. Out of respect and understanding for the well-being of the whole group, it was important to have some shape for the time I took to talk. To take up a lot of time was to deprive someone else of talking. But only occasionally did I feel like I had to really curtail what I had to say."

Pamela shepherded us well, allowing the occasional fizzy-bottle woman to speak longer that evening and encouraging the rest of us (by her example) to enfold that person. This holy woman managed to attend to the needs of all who were present, giving attention and time to everyone who wished to speak. She remained almost motionless, intently listening to each of us, although she often gently touched her holy adornment of silver-toned cuff bracelets as she gave her own insights—laced with self-disclaimers. We group members were lucky indeed to be introduced to this channel to God via imagination and discussion by our holy and earthy shepherdess Pamela.

TOUCHSTONES

HELD IN HEAVEN

Some of my meditations and dreams over the years have been so significant that they have become touchstones on my journey. Here are some of my most memorable shared imagination encounters—what I know of their meanings and what I'm still pondering.

In 1990, three years after giving birth to a healthy baby girl (our now-grown daughter), I miscarried when I was five months pregnant with another little girl. It had been a difficult pregnancy, with bleeding in the fourth month, which sent me to the hospital. But the bleeding had stopped, and the doctor had sent me home with the advice to treat myself gently, "like a cracked egg." However, in the fifth month, my amniotic fluid gushed out of me during a rehearsal at the Metropolitan Opera. I went right home and to bed. I still wasn't sure what was happening, because I had been leaking amniotic fluid for about a month, off and on. Sadly, the baby started coming in the middle of the night. My husband rushed me to the hospital, and I gave birth to a baby girl, who lived only a few hours.

The world seemed to stop turning. We named her Lily, after my mother's mother, who died much too young from cancer. Lily seemed like a beautiful but sad name for this little girl who didn't last long.

Several weeks after losing Lily, when I came back to being with people, I went to one of the women's spiritual direction meetings. During the quiet time, I found I was about to sob uncontrollably from sadness over losing Lily. I got up from my chair quickly, left the room, and cowered in a coat closet at the front of the church. I sobbed.

After a while, my sobs subsided a bit, and I heard Lily in my mind talking to me. She said, "Mommy, I want to talk to you."

I replied in my head, "Yes, sweetie, but I'm just so sad at losing you that I can hardly stop crying."

Lily spoke with a sweet voice. "I want to tell you about heaven, Mommy."

"Okay," I gasped, "tell me."

"They hold you, Mommy, they hold you."

Immediately, I had an image of tall, wise, angelic women in heaven passing Lily gently from one embrace to another, reveling in the beauty of this tiny little girl.

I cried again—but this time from joy.

I returned to the spiritual direction room and told my story to the women there. We shared tears and comfort together.

In the years since this meditation, this visit from Lily, I've thought about her words. I think now that they have a double meaning. She did mean that she was being held, because she knew that I worried that I had not held her long enough during her short time on earth. My arms had ached for weeks after the miscarriage from hugging a void. But I kept hearing the word "you" in her sentence, and I realize now that she was also saying that those tall, sacred women were holding *me* too. They were holding me in love and care as I was going through such sadness.

MARY PROMISES

Months later, as I was still grieving Lily's death, I had my most vivid, significant meditation. During the quiet time in a spiritual direction meeting, Mary, the mother of Jesus, showed up and talked with me!

Pamela, our group leader, had suggested that we all move from our usual cozy, library-like room into the church sanctuary for that evening's meeting. We were to ask Jesus to come and speak to us in meditation that night. But as I closed my eyes, Mary came forward in my mind, seeming to come right out of the huge Nativity window at the front of the church. She walked toward me and was crying, seemingly crying with me. I could see tears coming down the right side of her cheek.

Mary must have sensed my misgivings about seeing her instead of Jesus, because she said, as if to reassure me, "I'm not God." Then the mother of Jesus added, with the hint of a twinkle in her eye, "But I know him very well." I was still thinking about how this woman probably *did* know her own son very well, when Mary spoke directly to me, in a type of annunciation.

"You will be fruitful," she said, "like a tree planted by streams of water."

I knew that quotation was somewhere in the Bible, and I took the words to mean that I would be fruitful spiritually, and physically—with a child. I argued back because I was so devastated at having just lost a baby, and I couldn't bear the thought of false hope. "Don't promise me what you can't make happen," I told her rather forcefully.

Mary continued, "You will have a sweet son."

And then I saw him—a blond-headed little boy running toward me as I stood in front of a gray house.

I can't describe my amazement, wonder, and doubt. I had never thought much about Mary at all. In fact, I thought that "those Catholics" made too much of her. I had even joked about too much Marianism in the Catholic Church. And yet, there she was, crying with me and speaking words of promise to me. Those old beliefs fell completely away, and Mary became incredibly special to me from that moment on. I left the spiritual direction meeting stunned, amazed, and wondering.

The fulfillment of that encounter came about three years later, after my husband and I had decided to follow the path of adoption, leaving the gender of our baby-to-be in the hands of the adoption agency. On St. Patrick's Day, March 17, 1993, I picked up the phone and heard our caseworker tell me, "Baby boy is waiting for you here in Texas."

Tears just about shot out of my eyes! We flew to Texas and adopted our son at three weeks of age. As a boy, he *was* tow-headed (what we say in the South for blond), and we *did live* in a gray house!

I can't say enough about the importance of that meditation for me, not just because we did adopt a baby boy but because it opened me up to the incredible compassion of Mary. It's no wonder that centuries of people have felt drawn to her, especially in the ages when God and Jesus were seemingly becoming more distant, kinglike, and judging. Mary's nearness to humankind, her motherly compassion, and her own anguish in life made this woman so accessible to people who needed comforting. I haven't stopped reading about Mary, or thinking about her, or thanking her, or at times holding imaginative conversations with her. For me, she is an arrow that both embodies and points to the vast care, compassion, and courage of God the Mother.

I found the scripture that Mary had quoted to me a few years later as I applied to enter seminary to study spiritual direction. While writing my required spiritual autobiography, I was describing my "Mary meditation" and hoping to find the scripture she had quoted to me. I somehow knew it was a Psalm, so I decided to start from the beginning of the book of Psalms in the Bible and search until I found it. Well, there it was, immediately, in the very first Psalm!

> Blessed are those
> who do not follow the advice of the wicked

or take the path that sinners tread,
or sit in the seat of scoffers,
but their delight is in the law of the LORD,
and on that law they meditate day and night.
They are like trees planted by streams of water,
which yield their fruit in its season,
and their leaves do not wither.
In all that they do, they prosper."[51]

Amazement set in again, and the type of tears came that tell me to pay attention, because I'm going through deep spiritual waters. Over the years, Psalm 1 and this "annunciation from Mary meditation" have remained vivid and meaningful for me—experiences of a holy person I will forever treasure.

---

[51] Bruce M. Metzger and Roland E. Murphy, eds., *The New Oxford Annotated Bible, New Revised Standard Version* (NY: Oxford University Press, 1991), 675 OT.

SNAKE PEOPLE

Another spiritual touchstone was a dream that came to me in my first year of seminary. I'm still pondering its full meaning, but it was incredibly powerful and has something to do with a task I'm called to undertake.

The dream began with people coming up out of a muddy river bank; the mud was the color of sienna, a mixture of brown and orange. The people seemed to be part-human and part-serpent. These "snake people" were not at all frightening. In fact, there was incredible longing in their eyes as the individuals came toward me. It seemed as if each one had heard that I would make a place for him or her.

In the dream, I went to the president of some African nation and asked for a homeland for these people, but he refused. And more people kept coming out of that river.

The scene changed, and suddenly I was helping my young daughter Sarah to climb through the split-rail fence from our neighbor's yard into our front yard. As I put my arm around her, I could feel that her back was curved and covered with scales like a cobra. But she had feet, because I could see her little tennis shoes. We turned together toward home, and the dream ended.

Those nighttime images feel extremely significant to me, even decades later. Something still beckons me in the intense longing in those people's eyes. Sarah seemed so incredibly dear with her little tennis shoes, despite a back rounded and scaled like a serpent. I know it sounds bizarre and not appealing, but it was as if those people, including Sarah, were a type of being that I could understand extremely well, that I could care for in a very deep way.

Recently, after two women in writing class and critique group told me their own spiritual experience (in response to *my* stories), I suddenly understood who those snake people could represent—individuals who have shared imagination with the Divine. The words "serpent" and "spirit" contain many of the same letters, and water (the riverbed) is often linked to spirit—clues from my dream. Now I understand the imagery of those half-human, half-serpent creatures coming out of the river in my dream. I am one of them, and we are citizens of two worlds—the commonplace realm of physical reality and the domain of spirit with its loving messages from the Divine.

The scripture passage where Jesus counsels people to be "wise as serpents, innocent as doves" reminds me of those creatures in my dream. I see the longing in their eyes for a home, and I realize that I, too, have been seeking a spiritual home and have found it in many ways through the ever-enlarging idea of shared imagination. My hope is that, in writing this book, I can share my homeward spiritual journey and perhaps help other people come through the split-rail fence and find a home where Spirit and imagination dwell.

AFTERLIFE ISLAND

The music begins with two-note murmurs in the violins, depicting quietly lapping waves. Gently plucked string bass notes, distantly spaced, conjure up a boat rocking slowly on the water. A vast expanse appears in my mind, one of peace and gentleness.

Then the words start:

Soave sia il vento (May the winds be soft)
Tranquilla sia l'onda (May the waves be tranquil)
Ed ogni elemento (And may every element)
Benigno risponda (Respond kindly)
Ai nostri desir. (To our desires)[52]

The two heroines in Mozart's opera *Così Fan Tutte* are bidding goodbye to their lovers as the two men depart over the sea to war. By now, tears are streaming down my face, and I'm hoping against hope that the other musicians in the orchestra pit aren't noticing my tears or my foolish grin. My face feels as if it's shining, and I'm transported to another world.

Decades ago, when I first played *Così*, I decided that this short musical excerpt of the opera should be played at my funeral, for three reasons. First, the music is heartachingly beautiful. Second, the words express how I want to be sent off to the next world, with soft winds and tranquil waves. Finally, and most importantly, this is not a true

---

[52] W.A. Mozart, *Cosi Fan Tutte*, G. Schirmer's Collection of Opera Librettos (NY: G. Schirmer, Inc., 1951), 9.

farewell; the two lovers don't really leave. We listeners to this opera are in on the joke. These wager-making men are only pretending to leave and will return to their loved ones. Likewise, I believe that death is only a temporary parting.

Now, three months after watching my mother die slowly but peacefully in the hospital, I am overwhelmed with beauty and longing as this piece unfolds each night in the opera performance. This evening, as I play it, I see the colors and images of the afterlife. I envision a distant shore, undulating waves, and diamonds of sunlight sparkling off the water. The sea and sky shimmer with violet-blue and gold, painting a place of peace, joy, and beauty.

Then, in the twinkling of an eye, a heavenly turquoise blue appears, as an exquisitely unexpected chord settles like peace itself on the word *desir*. A few bars later, that breathtaking chord repeats on the same word, "desire." The whole landscape opens into something unknown and familiar at the same time—home.

Now, as the audience understands that the two lovers aren't really leaving, I smile, knowing more certainly than ever that neither is my mother really gone. I have seen that tranquil, sparkling island to which she traveled.

The music continues, and I imagine my own children playing a recording of this music at my funeral. I hope as they listen to the melodies that they, too, can see this shining world. May they envision me smiling wondrously at them and at that aqua-tinted vista of sea, sky, and shore.

The music finishes. I wipe my eyes, bid goodbye to Mom and that celestial home, and pray that my hands, lips, and breath can play flute for the next aria.

A RED VELVET PILLOW—WITH TASSELS!

Probably my most direct communication with the Divine came when I was the most upset—almost literally outside myself with dismay. It was the ninth of November, and I had just finished playing second flute and piccolo on *Carmen* for the Saturday matinee with the Metropolitan Opera. A decades-old conflict in the orchestra had reached an interior, unspoken, but very real tipping point for me.

I was unable to keep to my usual routine on a "double Saturday"—a day when I had to play both the matinee and the evening performance. I couldn't make myself eat at the cafeteria or nap in the cozy women's locker room. Phoning my best listeners resulted in unanswered calls. I had nowhere to go and no one to turn to.

Sitting alone and completely distraught on the usually comfortable cushions in the darkened orchestra women's locker room, I suddenly heard a voice in my head reminding me of a previous time when God seemed to speak to me.

The voice asked, "Remember when you were wondering if you should take early retirement from the MET, and I urged you to go to Pottery Barn? Remember how you saw the bunny statues where I said you'd find them? Go there again, to the left side of the store, and this time find a red velvet pillow."

"A red velvet pillow?" I sputtered to myself, disbelievingly.

The answer was immediate and emphatic. "Yes, with tassels!"

The words came faster than I could speak or write them, and the image of a red velvet pillow with a tassel on each corner popped into my mind just as rapidly. The added words "with tassels" seemed to mean extreme emphasis and reminded me of the old southern reply to an insult—"Same to you, with *knobs* on it!"

I sat for a long time, trying to remind myself that I was a rational person and that such an idea could come from my own imagination and my extreme emotional distress. But I couldn't rest, or eat, or talk to anyone, so I put on my coat, walked out of the MET, and started trudging north up Broadway.

As I walked, I talked to myself in my mind. "Be rational. If you *don't* find that pillow, it doesn't mean you can't take early retirement. And if you *do* find that pillow, it doesn't mean you have to take—"

The voice suddenly interrupted, "But if you find that pillow, will you believe I'm talking to you?"

Tears sprang to my eyes, because that voice in my head came so quickly and seemed so much like God. Was God speaking with me as I walked up Broadway, on a cloudy, pre-Christmas Saturday afternoon, surrounded by people rushing here and there? Either I was crazy, or this was really happening to me.

"Yes, I'll believe you're talking to me," I replied in my mind.

A block later, I arrived at Pottery Barn. In the front window, there was a red velour shawl with tassels, sitting under a matching velour pillow, without tassels. *Close*, I thought, *but not it.*

Next, inside the store, I spied a red velvet pillow with a reindeer embroidered on it in sequins—but no tassels. Then, halfway through the store, on the store's left-hand side, sitting on a big, beige sofa was the red velvet pillow, its four long tassels easily spotted against the neutral color of the couch.

Now I was barely keeping back sobs—tears always come to me when I'm in deep spiritual waters.

A young salesgirl approached. "Can I help you?"

Stroking the pillow, I managed to stumble out, "It's really beautiful."

"Yes, and we have one just like it in green on the other side of the store."

Of course, you do, I thought to myself, *because God told me to look on the left side.*

I somehow made my way out of the store and back to the MET. I even managed, a few hours later, to play the evening performance, although I can't tell you how well I played or even what the opera was. I was still shocked and wondering.

When I finally returned home that night, around half past midnight, my husband and I had our usual "catch up with each other" late-night talk. But this time I had quite a story to tell.

"So, where's the pillow?" my husband asked, totally believing my conversation with God.

"I didn't even think to buy it. I was so overcome by finding it."

"Well, on Monday, you should buy it and bring it home."

I did. And after much thought and talk with my husband and our daughter and son, I did take early retirement, about a year after that God conversation.

Years later, I asked one of my favorite artists, Ray Kleinlein, to paint a picture of that tasseled cushion. The resulting oil painting is beautiful—a cross between ultrarealism and impressionism—and it hangs in a place of honor in our home. A photo of the painting graces the cover of this book.

Although it has no inscribed title, that pillow painting sums up for me how God seems to work in my life. The Divine One never tells me exactly what to do, but She continually asks, "Will you believe I'm talking to you?"

A STUMBLING SPEECH

In addition to holding occasional imaginative conversations with God while walking, I once heard from the Divine when I tripped at a threshold! Let me tell the whole story. In the late 1990s, I followed Pamela Barnett's example and began working toward a master's degree in spiritual direction from the same school she had attended in New York City—General Theological Seminary. As I was about to graduate, I had three confidence-shaking conversations with three different priests. Maybe that's why God spoke so clearly to me on the day of my graduation.

At seminary, one clergyman and I had a private, spirited talk about whether experience should be a fourth leg of the traditional three-legged stool of Episcopal doctrine—along with scripture, reason, and tradition. I was maintaining the importance of experience, since I was beginning to trust the shared imagination and testing-the-fruits processes of the group. He was distrustful of experience, for whatever reasons, and preferred knowledge gained through academic study. So, at that meeting, he leaned closer to my face and asked rather condescendingly, "What do you think the Bible says about experience?"

I leaned back at him and said, "What do you think Paul thought about it? He certainly wasn't hit on the head by a *book* on the road to Damascus!"[53] We agreed to disagree about experience.

The next upsetting encounter happened at a church conference my husband and I were attending. At a coffee break during the conference,

---

[53] I refer to the disciple Paul's conversion experience of seeing a blinding light and hearing Jesus speak to him on the road to Damascus (Acts 9:1–19).

I mentioned to a priest we knew how I once explained the Christian concept of the Trinity to my Jewish friend Theresa. Theresa had been the first person who agreed to let me practice spiritual direction on her, a requirement while I was studying at seminary. I always used passages from the Hebrew scriptures to meditate on with her, and I never talked about Jesus in those sessions, in respect of her own faith tradition. However, one day outside of spiritual direction, she mentioned her unease with the more-than-one god idea she found in the Christian notion of the Trinity. So, I reached inside myself for some way to explain "three persons in one" and said that it might be like the element H_2O, which in one form is water, in another form is water vapor, and in another form is ice, but always the same element.

I thought that explanation was a bit inspired, but when this clergyman heard it, he said (in front of four or five other people), "Oh, that's the heresy of modalism." He offered no other explanation but turned to my husband and quipped, "Some people just flirt with heresy. Others marry it." I was stunned, hurt, and incredibly angry but said nothing. Saying nothing was my mistake.

My final encounter was even more spiritually painful. I really wanted at least one priest I knew well at my upcoming graduation, and I knew that the rector from my home parish in New Jersey would be out of town on my graduation day. So, I asked the rector from a parish in New York if he could attend my commencement ceremony. I knew and liked that clergyman and his female associate rector from attending weekday services at their church during my intensive semesters of seminary study in the summers.

The rector told me that both he and his associate would be busy the day of my commencement at an altar guild luncheon. I separately questioned the woman priest about whether she could be excused from the luncheon to attend my graduation. She seemed interested, but when the rector was informed, he refused to excuse her. So, I requested a consultation with the rector to explain why the presence of a personal friend/priest would mean a lot to me at the ceremony. He met with me but invited the associate without telling me she would be there.

At that meeting, the woman priest (who years later apologized to me for her words) chose to side with the rector and refused to attend my graduation because, as she told me, "I have to attend to the people put under my spiritual care."

So, who am I—some outsider? I thought. Persisting, I explained that I would value at least one clergy friend being at the ceremony, because I already felt like a second-class citizen at the seminary. I had studied in the looked-down-upon department called the Center for Christian Spirituality, and I had pursued a master of arts degree rather than the "preferred" ordination track.

The male priest then dumped on me the truckload of reasons why my degree and I were "not worse" (his words) but not the same as pursuing an ordination degree and becoming a clergy person. "The ordination degree takes three years," he said, "not merely the two years needed for your degree."

Actually, I thought to myself, *I've been studying part-time for six years, since I have to keep up my orchestra job and be a mother to two small children.* But I said nothing.

He intoned on. "The people who follow the master of divinity degree to ordination often leave home and job and family to come to the seminary," he said, seemingly suggesting that I was less committed to God.

Might not balancing job, family, and seminary be just as committed? I silently wondered.

"And," he continued, "the master of divinity degree is much more rigorous academically."

Well, I said in my mind, *I see that you're another clergyman who prefers books over experience.*

He pontificated on in that vein for what seemed like forever to me.

I was devastated. I cried almost daily for months and felt hurt for years over being told I was less than worthy to God. In hindsight, I see that I was in large part responsible for feeling so injured. Part of me had to believe that I really wasn't worthy enough to God, or the priest's comments would never have hurt for almost a decade. I also could have spoken up for myself as the priest detailed the superior glories of clerical education and ordination. Keeping silent and believing my second-class status were my mistakes.

God certainly tried to reassure me through meditations and

God-incidents—those times that are similar to what Jung called synchronicities—when a power higher than chance seems to work through a coincidence. I tried listening to that Godly reassurance. Amazingly, the clearest message came exactly at my seminary graduation. As I was entering the gorgeous cathedral-like church for the service, I was thrilled by the sound of the hundreds of people inside lifting their voices to God in song. But I tripped just a bit over the threshold at the entrance to the church, stumbling ever so slightly as I entered the sanctuary.

Then God said in my head, "The people who would keep you out of My House are no more an obstacle than that tiny, one-inch threshold. Next time, look down to notice them, then step over them and enter." Even at that moment, I knew that God was not telling me to look down upon my naysayers but simply not to be hurt by what I thought was their assessment of me as less than worthy to God. I see the blessing of this God-advice now, but I wish I had claimed it sooner and stopped feeling as if I were not quite acceptable to the Divine. The good news is that this difficult-to-grasp idea of God treasuring each of us was a thread that ran through our women's spiritual direction meetings, and eventually I learned to embrace being acceptable—heresies and all—to the Holy One.

DANCING ON THE TERRACE

I remember a vivid, pivotal meditation from my seminary days that came while I was attending a required silent group retreat at Holy Cross Monastery. That retreat/monastic house is beautifully situated on the Hudson River, just north of New York City, and its gorgeous setting should have been enough for me to enjoy being in silence. However, I was unused to long stretches of quiet time. Like a cranky child, I deliberately found ways to talk by calling home from the phone booth in the lobby and by buying something at the monastery bookstore so I could talk to the employee at the cash register! I knew I was supposed to be silent, but I exercised what I told myself was civil disobedience, just to survive.

I finally went to my small room and attempted to pray and meditate on where God was calling me at that point in my life. Surprisingly, a movielike story rolled out in my head, complete with characters, setting, and dialogue. It began as I was asked in my mind if I would dance with God. I balked, not feeling worthy to dance with the Almighty. "How about dancing with an angel?" the voice in my head asked. "Could you do that?"

"Yes," I replied and immediately saw myself dancing with different angels on a terrace outside a glittering ballroom at night. Inside the ballroom, "professional God-people" (priests, nuns, monks) were dancing with each other. I felt very much like Maria in the movie *The Sound of Music* as she danced with Captain Von Trapp's children outside an elegant party. Neither Maria nor I felt worthy to dance with the ballroom guests. Maria was only a servant; I was not studying toward ordination as a priest.

Suddenly, Jesus cut in on my dancing with the angels, just as Captain Von Trapp had cut in as Maria danced with his children. Jesus and I looked into each other's eyes, and I found an incredible power in his gaze. I felt very much like Maria staring into the captain's eyes. I was stunned and shy.

Jesus asked if we could walk and talk together, and I agreed. As we walked in the moonlight, he asked me to recall the flute lesson I had just given to Jean, one of my favorite students.

"Oh, that was so much fun!" I exclaimed. "She's only in high school, but she's so talented and so musical! I helped her to play more beautifully some difficult etudes by the French composer Jeanjean."

"Do you notice the similarities between her name and the composer's name—Jean and Jeanjean?" Jesus asked. "What do you think that means?"

"Maybe in some way I was helping her become more herself?" I ventured as an answer.

"You're good at that, Mary Ann. You're good at helping people become more their true selves. Do you think you could do that for me?" Jesus queried.

"Do you mean, could I be a spiritual director? Are you asking me to be that? Yes, yes, I'd love to do that!" I answered, relieved that what I was studying to become was also what God was asking of me.

Jesus silently beamed, the movie/meditation ended, and I was left feeling almost levitated off the floor with the joy of being asked to do what I already loved doing—spiritual direction.

The good news of my movielike meditation seems to be that God loves us all equally and calls us deliberately to different professions and life passions. Even when we feel unworthy to dance with the elite in the ballroom, God cuts in to dance with us, to walk and talk with us, and to invite us to God's longing for us—which is most often our deepest heart's desire also. Thanks, Jesus, for cutting in as I danced on the terrace.

GANESHA RISES

Trust God (and my imagination) to send me a parable containing the Hindu deity Ganesha while sitting within a circle of meditating Christian women! The Divine One must have a wacky sense of humor.

Everything was very ordinary that evening as we women gathered to meditate and talk with each other at our weekly spiritual direction meeting at church. In the quiet time that evening, I asked God for help with my son, who had not liked high school and who didn't want to attend any college full-time.

Jesus said to me, "Let me tell you a parable. There once was a mother who worked very hard, rowing her son in a small boat across a lake to the shore of adult responsibility."

Yeah, that's me, I thought, *but what's next? What else can I do?*

Jesus continued his parable. "Once the two of them arrived at that shoreline, nothing happened, so the mother rowed them back to the first side of the lake, where the journey had begun, and started all over again, propelling the vessel and her son to the far shore."

Oh great, more work for me. I inwardly sighed. But I could visualize myself rowing halfway across the lake on a second trip.

Suddenly, the elephant-headed Hindu god Ganesha began to rise up out of the water, looking for all the world like Esther Williams[54] in an old movie, surging up with fountains spurting all around. I was amazed and baffled.

I knew about Ganesha from teaching Religion 101 at the men's

---

[54] In the 1940s and 1950s, Esther Williams starred in movies that featured amazingly choreographed swimming and diving scenes.

college where I lived and worked. That deity represents good luck, prosperity, and second chances.

I was still reeling from the surprise of the Ganesha/Esther Williams figure when a real Indian elephant, bedecked with jewels, rose out of the lake. Immediately, my son leaped from our rowboat, jumped on the back of the elephant, and, together with a young woman behind him, rode that regally attired animal to the distant shore. *What does that mean?* I wondered to myself.

I didn't tell my meditation story right away that evening. As the leader of the group, I quite properly let the other women speak first about their own experiences. But eventually, I did recount the unexpected parable. I was a bit apprehensive as to how the group would react.

"Maybe your son will marry a young girl from India!" one woman exclaimed.

"Maybe, but my best guess is that this parable is more symbolic. I think my son will find his way to adulthood in a manner that is quite foreign to me (like Ganesha) but nevertheless quite splendid (like the bejeweled elephant). There may be a young woman involved in helping him. There might even be an element of good luck and second chances in my young man's journey."

Another woman chuckled. "I was pretty surprised that Jesus would send a story about a Hindu god in a Christian meditation, but now it makes sense. Wow!"

Wow, indeed, I thought in amazement.

WHEN CHATTY KATHY MADE ALL SHIMMER

One bright spring afternoon, a time of quiet and an abundance of light opened the shared imagination window in surprising ways. I was leading a women's quiet afternoon at one of the loveliest spots I can think of—a friend's house in the Virginia countryside. Her home is simple and not large, but it is oriented in such a way that most of the glass is on its south-facing side to maximize the sunlight. Every vista inside and outside the house lends itself to pondering beauty. It is a place where one feels blessed by loveliness, light, and quiet.

This particular afternoon, I explained to the dozen or so women the topic of the quiet period, then encouraged them to sit inside or outside the house, or to wander the grounds, and to think, meditate, or write about what might come up for them during the hour of silence.

As soon as I had finished introducing the theme for the day, I closed my eyes to try meditating myself. Immediately, the Holy Spirit as a female presence started chattering in my left ear. The name "Chatty Kathy" sprang to mind, because it really seemed as if Sister Holy Spirit had so much to say that she just couldn't stop talking. Her main point came very early in the talk. "Write your book and call it *Shared Imagination: A Memoir*."

"A memoir? Why a memoir?" I believed I was supposed to write about the process of forming and running a women's spiritual direction group. "Why should I write about my own life, about my own experiences, my own story? I'm not that special."

"Everyone has a story. Tell yours."

How characteristic of the Divine. She did not tell me I was special.

She simply stated that everyone has a story. I calmed down a bit, but I still didn't like the idea of writing about myself.

At one point in the meditation, Chatty Kathy Holy Spirit suggested that I go outside to the little fenced-in garden by the back door. Obediently, I went outside, sat on a low brick wall, and gazed. A tall, homemade trellis riveted my attention. It was freestanding, four-sided, and made of branches wired together to form a tall pyramid shape. I knew that my friend's husband and their son had crafted the trellis by hand, working on it together. Its rustic beauty held the promise of more splendor as the beans planted at its base would clamber up and bloom on those supporting branches.

"Look," directed Holy Spirit, "this is a rather humble object, but *it is not ordinary.*"

And as I looked, everything around and within that pyramid trellis shimmered with light and inner meaning. The sunshine indeed was bright, and the air seemed crystal clear, but there was more to it than that. The trellis took on meaning as something of great beauty made lovingly by a father and son working together. The seemingly ordinary object had become extraordinary.

Indeed, wherever I looked in that small, lovely garden, each object shimmered with inner meaning and seemed suffused with the holy bursting just below the surface of the commonplace. All things shimmered. It was numinous—quite a slice of exalted awareness.

Holy Spirit was showing me that everything, even that handmade trellis, is simply stuffed with inner significance to God and to those who look with spiritual eyes. She was counseling me that my very ordinary stories could also shimmer with mystical meaning.

In the days, weeks, and months since that experience, I have sometimes despaired over writing this book as a collection of stories and over writing this book at all. But when I remember that bright afternoon in the garden and the brilliant light that shimmered everywhere I looked, I take heart and start writing again.

SHARING LIFE'S MOMENTS

A REVERENT PET

Shared imagination is still working in my life, sometimes in unexpected ways, and I often borrow other women's meditations or real-life experiences as spiritual keepsakes for myself. Leslie's true tale of a keenly perceptive canine will stick with me not only as a dog-incident but also (turning the word "dog" around) as a God-incident, an experience where the Divine seemed present.

Leslie, an old friend from my previous church in Virginia, called me unexpectedly one day to talk about things that were bothering her spiritually. We shared many stories and experiences together over the phone but ended with her telling me about a woman and a faithful dog.

Leslie began her tale: "An elderly friend, Jennifer, had often told me how she missed kneeling during prayers. Her church habitually stood while praying, and she wanted to kneel but didn't want to be the only one on her knees." Laughing, Leslie continued, "Since Jennifer suffered from Alzheimer's, she told me that story many, many times. Well, Jennifer eventually died, and her daughter brought her deceased mother's service dog, Ginger, to the funeral service. That dog had been such a godsend during the last years of Jennifer's life."

Leslie went on, "I was sitting at the aisle during the service and had a good view of Ginger, who sat obediently in the aisle at the front pew, next to the daughter. During the funeral service, Ginger would instinctively stand when the congregation stood and sit when the people would sit down. But during the prayers, I wondered if I should kneel in deference to Jennifer's long-standing desire to be on her knees when praying. Just as I was trying to decide what to do, I looked down the aisle to Ginger, who, although the congregation was standing, suddenly prostrated her doggy self on the floor of the church!"

Tears of surprise, happiness, and spiritual sharing sprang to my eyes as I heard the end of this dog tale. I could see in my mind's eye Ginger performing the kneeling that her mistress would have wanted, right at that prayer moment in the funeral service. My dear friend Leslie brought me not a shaggy dog tale but a true God-incident and a moment of shared imagination, wonder, and joy.

A GOOD JOKE THAT DIDN'T DIE

We couldn't be more different, Melinda and I, but I learned to love her and her raucous, self-deprecating humor, especially when she told stories of her own spiritual experiences. Big-boned and always dressed in loose-fitting clothes, she contrasted with my obsession to look slim and fashionably dressed at all times. She was an artist who decorated the walls of her house with things like partially melted vinyl records, scratched on with a pencil. I preferred Laura Ashley florals and mini-prints in my oh-so-properly furnished home. But Melinda had a deep vein of spirituality and could make all of us laugh when she wanted to. This earthy raconteur told us her funniest story one evening during a spiritual direction meeting.

She began, "I just got back yesterday from visiting my father in California. He's dying, and I was dreading this visit. On the airplane going out there, I kept going over all the advice you ladies had given me at our last meeting: Dying people might see departed loved ones and even have conversations with them. It's important to validate their experiences. I was priming myself for whatever strange things Dad might say or do. When I got to his house, he was in a hospital bed in the living room, looking really thin and pale and hooked up to all kinds of machines. My sister and brother and I exchanged worried looks and verbally tiptoed around the fact that Dad was dying.

"Suddenly, Dad tolls in a deep voice, 'Ask me the question.'

"*Oh God*, I'm thinking, *this is it. He wants me to ask him some important, end-of-life question. He's going to talk about seeing dead people. Oh God, I don't know what to ask him. I don't know what he'll answer. I don't know how to handle this.*

"But I ask him, 'What question, Dad?'

"'Ask me how I'm doing.'

"'Okay, Dad. How are you doing?'

"Dad shrugs. *I make a living.*"

We women in the circle doubled over laughing as Melinda continued, "He made a joke! He deliberately made a joke to lighten everybody's mood. He knew he was dying. We knew it too. But he made it easier for all of us. What a gift!"

What a treasure this woman was to our group. And what a gift it continues to be to imaginatively experience another's spiritual encounters through sharing stories.

A PEACEFUL NIGHT AND A PERFECT END

During my recent visit with Emily, she told me of the night her husband died. It was such a moving story that I asked if I could record her tale and use it to help others. As she recounted her memories, I was struck by how many details she remembered and how graphically I could enter into those last months and the final night of her husband's life. To me, it was a beautiful example of shared imagination. I was reminded of the opening words of the evening prayer service of Compline with which our group closed each gathering—"The Lord Almighty grant us a peaceful night and a perfect end. Amen."[55] Emily's story contained much that wasn't serene, but the end certainly seemed peaceful and perfect.

I began, "I know this will be difficult, to talk about that night."

Emily interrupted, "No, it's not hard at all to talk about my husband's death. The background of his medical troubles makes that night a blessing. For a long time, he had been having a great deal of trouble. He wasn't able to sleep in his bed. He'd sleep on the sofa, so he could keep his foot on the floor, because his circulation was bothering him.

"Then came the time when he came up to me and said, 'I don't know what's wrong; my pants leg is all wet.' I replied that he must have spilled water when he was washing dishes. So, he changed his sweat suit and put on another one, but about twenty minutes later, his pants leg was wet again. We looked and realized that the serum was seeping through his skin. It wasn't blood; it was the clear liquid part of blood. We learned

---

[55] *The Book of Common Prayer, according to the use of The Episcopal Church* (The Church Hymnal Corporation and Seabury Press, 1977), 127.

from the doctor that Rob's blood was circulating to his feet, but it did not have enough strength to come back up to his heart. After that, Rob was doing more walking at the rec center and telling his doctor that he was 'just fine, just fine!' He had a good December and a wonderful Christmas. The family was here, and we had a glorious time together.

"But in January, this brave fighter started to fail. He had three or four different doctors talking to him. One thought he might have cancer of the blood and should have injections every week and a spinal tap. I could just see my husband not resonating with this proposed treatment. So, I asked him, 'What do you want to do?' He answered, 'I'm not going back to that doctor. This is ridiculous.' So, January continued with lots of doctor appointments. My husband was going to the wound clinic to have his leg wrapped and get various treatments, and to his primary doctor for his regular medications, and to another doctor for COPD, because he wasn't breathing well. They wouldn't give him oxygen because his breathing level wasn't lower than eighty, but we finally got oxygen that he could have overnight while he slept. He was going downhill and got very bad by the end of January. He didn't want to get up and didn't want to eat. Our daughter bought a machine that would grind up all his food so it was palatable for him to drink, but he wasn't even interested in that.

"On that last day, our daughter was here at our house and said, 'Mom, I think we really need to go to the emergency room.' I agreed, so we called the rescue squad. They had to bring in a stretcher to take my husband out of the house. Our daughter was overseeing getting her dad out of the house while I was looking for his Social Security card and what not. When we got to the emergency room, there wasn't a hospital bed available at that moment. While we waited, they x-rayed Rob and gave him special inhalation so he could get oxygen, but he was very uncomfortable.

"Finally, a bed was available. They moved Rob to a gurney that they could roll into the hospital room. I was walking into that room loaded down with his coat, my coat, my purse, and everything, because I was going to spend the night there, in the chair by the bed. I got near the bed, on one side of it, while the nurses were on the other side, getting Rob ready to move him to the hospital bed. One of the nurses was fiddling with the oxygen, preparing to have that transferred to Rob. But as they lifted him and the sheet onto the bed, one of the nurses said, 'He's stopped breathing!' And the doctor said, 'His heart has stopped.' I was standing there with our daughter. I was startled and grabbed Rob's hand. I saw that his eyelids weren't totally closed; I could see a little slit of his eyes. I felt compelled to take my hand and close his eyelids and straighten his head so it was supported by the pillow.

"Then I felt this overwhelming sense of joy that my lifelong companion was safe. I knew that the following week Rob had three terrible medical appointments scheduled, including one with the vascular surgeon. I was afraid they were going to have to amputate his leg. I knew it was going to be a dreadful time for my husband. I thought, *Thank you, God. You have saved him from this terrible future, and you're taking him home.* I just felt such a peaceful moment of resolve and of joy.

"When the doctor asked if I wanted him to resuscitate Rob, I got a little angry and said, 'What? Bring him back so he can suffer again? No!' Our poor daughter, sitting beside me, wanted to say, 'Yes, yes, yes.' But Rob and I had had the discussion of how we wanted our end of life to be. To me, that moment was beautiful, it was quiet, it was serene. And I've carried those feelings ever since. I have not been a mourning widow. I feel joy for him, that he's singing tenor in the celestial choir, saving a seat in the alto section for me. I have felt a sense of gratitude. That's the way I feel about that night."

As Emily finished speaking, I realized again the value of shared imagination through the telling of life stories, the recounting of God-incidences—those times when one senses the presence of God in one's daily, earthly life. Emily's tale is now a treasured touchstone of my own that I can bring to mind anytime I feel the need to experience trust and gratitude in life's dark moments.

THE RIGHT ROAD

Telling our stories to each other seems essential to our well-being as humans and can even be a type of prayer. Theologian Marjorie Procter-Smith writes, "Telling one's story in the community is telling it to God."[56] Relating our important memories also involves shared imagination as the listeners put themselves imaginatively and emotionally into the scenes described.

Melinda, our insightful member with a sense of humor, shared with me a story within a story as I was writing my master's thesis about our meditation group. Beginning with her journal entry about one of our meeting's meditations, her tale moved to a wonderful, almost archetypal story about her mother, then returned to her own quest for a path to God.

Melinda began, "I remember we were meditating on stories of the kingdom of God in the Bible, like buying the field with the treasure in it and buying the pearl of great price (Matt 13: 44–46). One of the questions Pamela asked us was where our treasure was. So, on that night, I wrote:

> 'The things I value the most—my art, my husband, my kids—are the things that force me to push deepest into myself and to come closest to my intuition and to God to make them work. All these things that I most value falter the further I get from myself and from God. There (in God) is the strength. There is the source of any love I have.

---

[56] Marjorie Procter-Smith, *Praying with Our Eyes Open* (Nashville: Abingdon Press, 1995), 59.

'Help me, God, to love out of purity and strength, rather than from fear and detachment. Help me to love myself with strength, not just protect myself out of fear.

'What I need to know is that I'm looking in the right places for the right things. These stories say you can find the kingdom of God by happenstance, or by looking for it, or by casting out a net, or by becoming a disciple of the Lord and looking within. I'll search forever and go on and on as long as I'm reassured *I'm on the right road*.'"

Melinda looked up from her reading. "See, that's what this group was constantly reassuring us: that God is the place to look. It reminds me of a story about my mother when she was a young actress in New York City. She was dating a guy who invited her up to his house in the Bronx. She wore her little dancing slippers and her fancy little dress and had dinner with him at his house in the Bronx. Then they said good night, and she walked out of his house onto the street.

"Suddenly she realized that she didn't have a nickel for the subway. But there she was, standing on Broadway, and her apartment was on Broadway, all the way down in the Village. So, she said to herself, 'Here's Broadway. I'll just walk down Broadway.'

"She walked all night, and by the time she got to her apartment, her little dancing shoes were in tatters. That's a long walk, probably twelve miles!

"But I'm thinking, in my own spiritual journey, I can be like my mother when she walked all the way down Broadway from the Bronx to the south end of Manhattan. She walked all night, because she knew she was on the right road and eventually she'd get home. As long as I know I'm on the right path, I'll put up with any problems along the way."

Melinda's tale has forever etched its pictures into my mind and heart. I'm so grateful to Melinda for recounting the story and for giving me the opportunity to live it in my mind through shared imagination.

JESUS WEARS A BACKPACK

Recently, Carla, a wonderful woman from one of my groups, not only reminded me of a meditation of hers but also related the life events that she believes resulted from that meditation. First, Carla described the background situation of her imaginative encounter:

"The backpack meditation was very important to me and continues to be so. I had that meditation at a time when my son Harry, who had been diagnosed with ADHD when he was five, was struggling in middle school. He was having problems behaviorally as well as academically, and I was just at a loss of what to do. As you recall, Mary Ann, I often have vivid meditations, and I mean crazily vivid, which is wonderful. During that particular meditation, while asking for guidance, I saw (in my imagination) Harry sitting at a desk in a middle school classroom. Then I scanned over and saw Jesus sitting next to him with my son's backpack on! Harry seemed mildly annoyed that Jesus was there, but he accepted it. They both got up to go to the next class, and Harry looked over at Jesus and beckoned him to follow, reluctantly of course, but making eye contact with Jesus as if to say, 'Come on, come on, let's go.' And then I saw them walking down the hall together."

As Carla paused, I remembered that meeting night and that graphic, imaginative picture she told us of Jesus trudging behind the young man down the halls of a middle school, carrying the boy's backpack. It was a wonderful, wacky, visual reminder to me of God's constant care for us.

Carla went on to explain what she learned, what she calls her "takeaway," from that imagining. "When I came out of that meditation in the group, I realized and was reminded again that Harry was being *guided* and that he *wasn't alone*. I've had many similar reminders since then, which is okay, because we don't always hear God clearly the first time, do we? At that particular period in my life, I was feeling completely overwhelmed and immersed with trying to fix Harry's problems at school. Teachers were calling me with advice on how to handle him. I felt way out of my league because I didn't know about middle schoolers; I taught college students. I was completely overwhelmed. But that meditation reminded me that I wasn't alone in this situation. I experienced that kind of 'peace that passes understanding,'[57] which is my theme for many of my imaginative encounters. Of course, like all humans, it's hard for me to hang on to that peace. But I would come out of countless contemplative scenes and stories with a sense that not only were things going to be okay, but *everything was okay at that moment.* Those meditations were a way to remind me that I was not walking by myself. The scene of Jesus ambling behind Harry down the corridors of the middle school, carrying my son's backpack, was hugely important at that time and even more significant recently."

Carla then told me about current experiences in Harry's life that reminded her of the backpack meditation. "Harry has grown into a lovely young man. He always seemed very unique to me in many ways and still has a very high emotional intelligence. Like any teen, he doesn't always make the best decisions, but he has this really strong connection to other humans.

"A few months ago, Harry got his driver's license, but he has had four driving incidents that have tested him. One was when he was speeding down a residential road, zooming by one of my colleagues from college. That coworker of mine followed Harry to the house he was visiting, pulled him aside and had a very serious, good conversation with him about driving too fast. For me, there's the backpack from my meditation. It wasn't Jesus following Harry, but it was a colleague of mine, who took the time to have that talk with him.

"Two weeks later was Harry's high school graduation, and he found himself at a party afterwards, where he didn't know there was going to be drinking. He ended up sitting all night long with his friends who

---

[57] *The Book of Common Prayer, according to the use of The Episcopal Church* (The Church Hymnal Corporation and Seabury Press, 1977), 339.

were drunk, taking care of them until he could drive everyone home safely the next morning."

Hardly pausing for breath, Carla then related more encounters that reminded her of God's guidance for her son. "A week later, Harry was at another gathering, a *family* gathering, where his friend who lived at that house became very intoxicated. Some of Harry's other friends at the celebration became very uncomfortable, so my son chose to leave the party and drive three of his friends home. He was making really amazing choices, which brought to me that backpack meditation.

"Most recently, Harry called me and said he had been pulled over going 38 miles per hour in a 35 mph zone. It seemed a bit ridiculous to me, but I didn't tell him that. I told him that he was pulled over not because he was doing something terrible but maybe because he was a young man driving in a small town, or maybe the policeman had seen him speeding another time, or maybe the cop had seen other drivers speeding on that stretch of road and pulled Harry over as an example to others. I explained that he was pulled over because he is (and all of us are) extremely connected to all other human beings. Harry seemed to understand. For me, it was another example of difficult experiences that turned out very positive for my son in the long run. I believe those incidents are that backpack.

"It's scary to put your kid out on the road when he may not have developed enough to always make great choices, but *I do believe he's being guided.* I've even talked to Harry about this. I've told him, 'When you're not sure what to do, say a prayer and ask for guidance.' I even told my boy about the backpack meditation at the time I experienced it. He was in sixth grade and thought it was weird but good. That's what he said: 'That's kind of weird, Mom, but it's good.' Ha, ha!"

I loved hearing Carla's meditation again, and the real-life stories that followed it. I told her, "Let me see if I can sum this up in a way that seems right to you. In all these stories, *human beings* were acting, guiding, and being guided, but behind the human actions you find the *divine guidance,* and you remember the image of Jesus carrying Harry's backpack?"

"Absolutely," Carla replied. "As Harry gets older, it may be that Jesus has to carry a *briefcase* or something else, but I know He will be there for my son. What I glean from almost all of my own meditations is the reminder that God is always present. I think one of my weaknesses is not remembering that fact and letting worry take over instead. I think—and I mean this from the bottom of my heart—that my experience with the meditation group has given me what I need—very vivid reminders—not just words—but very visual, graphic reminders that the Holy One is always present."

The reassurance that God is with us *now and in the future* is one of the most wonderful outcomes of the imaginative encounters with the Divine we women experienced in our gatherings. Hearing the resulting life incidences where God seemed to be working, or "God-incidences" as we sometimes called them, is another way to experience the joy of shared imagination.

CONVERSATIONS, DREAMS, AND LETTERS

A VARIETY OF ANGELS

Because I've come to trust sharing imagination with the Divine, I sometimes find myself having imaginative conversations with God, occasionally even while I'm driving. That might sound a bit scary to other motorists, but the conversations don't happen that often, and they never seem to distract me from driving. Here are two examples of short but reassuring traveling conversations with the Holy One.

I am very fond of the idea of angels, of having angels watching over me, protecting me, guiding me, and so on. For years, I have noticed that when I need to find something, I usually get help by consulting "the finding angels." The term "finding angel" is of my own making, and I have come to think that many such angels surround me, since I need help finding things so often.

I also like the idea of having guardian angels—even imagining the names Rosamunda and Chiara as my own guardian angels. I also seem to collect images of angels. One day, while sitting in my music/meditation room, I observed just how many statues or pictures of angels I had on display, something I had never noticed before. Just then, I felt led to look inside the small guitar I had bought for my son the previous Christmas, which was tilted against the wall in a corner. Leaning forward, I peered in and saw the brand name—"Angelique." *Okay*, I thought, *I must really be drawn to angels!*

A woman in church warned me that a fascination with angels might get in the way of worshipping God. She even quoted some Bible passage (Hebrews 1:5–2:18) about the importance of putting Jesus before celestial messengers. Then I became troubled about my fondness for these heavenly beings.

So, I asked God about angels one day while driving on a familiar stretch of road where I had no turns to make for quite a while. God seemed to start up a conversation with me.

God began, "Mary Ann, don't you love colors, especially the color red?"

I answered, "Yes, you know I love red; it's my favorite color."

God continued, "Well, what if there was only one type of red and not the vast spectrum of reds that exist? And what about flowers? What if there was only one type of flower to enjoy? And remember how much you and your mother loved seeing and touching fabrics? A fabric store was more fun than a candy store for the two of you. What if there was only one type of fabric to see and touch?"

Suddenly, I could see in my mind a spectrum of red hues, a wide variety of flower species, and a multitude of fabric colors and textures.

God pressed on. "Angels are like that, Mary Ann. There are many kinds of wonderful angels, and they are no more dangerous to enjoy than enjoying myriads of colors, flowers, or fabrics."

I felt immensely better about my fondness for angels, and I still enjoy reds, flowers, and fabrics!

Another time, I was feeling troubled about my training in Reiki—an Asian hands-on healing technique. The process involves placing one's hands in certain positions on or over another's body and channeling divine healing through oneself to the other person. I believed in the process, mostly because my hands heated up whenever I practiced the method. However, I was conflicted at inwardly invoking some of the names of heavenly helpers that I had been taught in my Reiki initiation.

I asked God, "Who are these beings?"

Before I could finish my question, I heard God answer, quite clearly and suddenly: "Nurses!"

I understood that one-word reply to mean that a multitude of angels exist, and some celestial beings have special healing powers, much like nurses on earth. I was comforted by both conversations. Each helped me to understand that I was not straying from my Christian beliefs by practicing that ancient healing technique or by a fondness for angels.

THE SPY GUY DREAM

During a time when I was moving to North Carolina from Virginia and packing up no-longer-needed household items to give to my son in Baltimore, I shared imagination with the Divine in an *espionage adventure dream.* In the dream, I was trying to get back to some part of a city. A few college students were a distance behind me and also wanted to get to that place, but they seemed too afraid to try the journey. I crossed the street and started to look for the path by myself. I was a bit scared, because it was dark, and by then, I was alone and couldn't quite remember the way.

All at once, the spy guy was with me, and he told me that what we had witnessed by accident a few nights ago was actually a thief putting money into the pope's bank. Quite firmly, he stated, "You know what we have to do."

I *did not* know what he meant, but suddenly he and I were breaking into the pope's house! The spy guy seemed to know just how to get into His Holiness's residence. Once inside, this secret agent deciphered some clue in the wall decoration, then went to a desk and started pushing a button in the far right corner of the wall that would wake up the pontiff.

Guards began to arrive. I was scared that they would shoot or arrest us. I got on the ground, almost prostrate, and said to the guards, "We just need to see the Holy Father."

Unexpectedly, an oily, dishonest-looking man entered the room, opened the pontiff's vault, and took out some papers. Some of the safe's contents looked like the paper jackets for 33 rpm vinyl records, but on the top of the stack were smaller items resembling sleeves for 45 rpm records. They were dark green with gold embossing on them.

The bad guy gloated at us, "Look, this was all that was in the safe." He was saying that we were wrong, that a thief had *not* put money in the pope's safe a few evenings ago.

Suddenly, an idea popped into my head, and I told this evil man, "Run your finger over the gold on those record sleeves."

He did what I suggested, and real 14-karat gold leaf came off on his fingers. The spy guy and I were vindicated! The gold leaf was the way this bad guy was hiding that precious metal in the pope's vault. We had caught the thief. We were not shot or arrested. The whole thing seemed so much like the end of some spy novel—at the very last minute, the good guys won, and the dream ended.

The next morning, during my meditation on the dream, God began explaining the nighttime vision to me. "You and the secret agent are the good guys here," God said, "and the unctuous guy you have met in real life: he typifies the people who have been dishonest and unkind to you in recent months. But you will overcome. That's the whole point of the dream. I thought it was quite a nice touch to make it a spy novel, the kind your husband loves to read. I thought he might actually enjoy your dream through the espionage novel genre."

Wanting more, I asked, "Is there anything else you'd like to tell me about the dream?"

Obligingly, God replied, "Sure. The students represent people who are afraid and unable to move toward what they want in life. You are also afraid, but you keep moving in the direction of your dreams. The gold is the time and effort of God's love. It doesn't belong in a vault, even the pope's safe, or being stolen by a few. It belongs to all people, as you and the spy guy were trying to rectify in the dream. It needs to come out of that locked place and go to its rightful owners—you and the whole world. It really is my love, and you two are trying to free it, while some people would hide it, misuse it, dote on it as their own, keep it from others, keep it locked up 'safe' as only theirs. Do you understand?"

Mentally scratching my head, I admitted, "Not quite, but I'm trying. The gold is your love, and it needs to be free, and others would encapsulate it into the wrong things, into things where it can't be seen or shared as your love?"

"Bingo. You've got it. Now keep carrying on. You still have some work to do. Be of good cheer, my daughter. I am with you. Always."

"Who is the spy guy?"

Chuckling, Jesus joined the conversation. "Me, of course. I am with you in this and always. Walk, talk, laugh, dream! This love belongs to you and to the whole world. Now go, sweetie. Let's get on to this road trip to see your son. He and his girlfriend are waiting for you."

"One more question about the spy guy dream," I continued. "Who is the pope, and why is the money in his safe?"

God the Father answered this time. "I don't like to say this, but sometimes my own people are the ones who would take my love away from others. I'm not blaming the pope or the Catholic Church literally. It's a bigger metaphor for all who call themselves my people. They need to be careful how they spend or hoard my love. It is for all, not just a few, not just those who 'believe rightly,' not those who are in the correct group or color or creed or dogma or time or place. Be careful, my children, and do not steal my love from others and then hoard it in the church. It will break free. It must. It is made to share with and spread to *all*. Do not be on the wrong side of this issue, for I will cause my love to break free, and you would be wise not to get in its way."

"Thank you for explaining things, God. Now it's time for our last church service here in Virginia. It will be very emotional with the Celtic Farewell the congregation is saying over us. Help me and my husband play our music well."

"You will."

DRIVING WITH MARY

I'm alone in the car, driving on a four-hour trip, when music opens a window to the Holy. The familiar melody of one of my favorite opera scenes catches my attention from the car radio. Instead of shuttling back and forth between a news channel and pop Christmas tunes, I settle in to listen to the opera's gorgeous strains. The performance sounds like the Metropolitan Opera Orchestra; the flutes are stressing exactly the notes I remember James Levine asking us to emphasize when I played this opera under his conducting. The English horn and the piccolo resonate with the same tone colors of the players with whom I worked during my years in that orchestra. I can't place the soprano, but she's singing exquisitely, with a clear, sparkling tone in the high notes and a gorgeously darker color in the low ones. Once again, I'm totally entranced by the "Willow Song" and the following "Ave Maria" from Verdi's opera *Otello*.[58]

I'm mesmerized by this rendition, relishing every nuance and color of the performance as well as the sadness that is palpable as the opera's heroine, Desdemona, sings and prays on what she suspects is her last night on earth. She intones a folk song about a girl named Barbara, dying from the grief of being abandoned by her lover and predicting that willow branches will be her funeral garland. Turning to prayer, Desdemona asks Mary to pray for all of us—for the sinner as well as the innocent, for the powerful as well as those brought low by oppression. Repeatedly, Desdemona asks Mary to pray for us *nell'ora della morte*—at

---

[58] Giuseppe Verdi and Arrigo Boito, *Otello*, vocal score (NY: G. Ricordi and Co, 1924), 328–333, 338–341.

the hour of our death. Her final *Ave* soars to an exquisitely soft, high A-flat, then swoops down more than an octave to an almost whispered *amen*. As the violins disappear into the heavens on their final soft high note, tears are streaming down my face at the exalted beauty of this music, and I grip the steering wheel to stay safe on this relatively open stretch of interstate highway. Memories well up inside me.

Tears—my own road sign of entering deep spiritual waters—begin to flow. I remember learning to pay attention to my tears from my Women's Spirituality professor at seminary. I also remember Mary— how much she has come to mean to me over the past two decades, ever since her first unexpected appearance to me while I was meditating in a women's group ("Mary Promises" in this book). That evening, she seemed to come right out of the stained glass Nativity window in the church; she cried with me over my miscarriage of a baby girl, and she promised me spiritual and physical fruitfulness. The baby boy she foretold is in his twenties now.

I reminisce about how many books I've read about Mary since then and how much I've learned about her attraction to so many individuals over the centuries. Mary has always been revered as a sympathetic and compassionate mediator, especially in the times when God seemed more and more distant and judgmental. In past centuries, Mary's acceptance of becoming Jesus's mother was viewed as praiseworthy feminine submission. These days, feminist theologians write about Mary's extraordinary strength in her willingness to become pregnant before marriage. I love this holy woman for all the characteristics I've discovered about her.

On the car radio, another beautiful excerpt brings me back to the present. This time, the piece is unfamiliar to me, but it seems as mystical as the *Otello* selections. I press the info button on the radio and discover that this music is also about meeting death—a setting of the *Nunc Dimitis* (Luke 2:25–35)—where an elderly Hebrew prophet welcomes the end of his life because he has seen God's salvation in a special child. Suddenly, I'm reliving my mother's death in 2000 and my father's passing, six years later.

Then, Mary seems to put words in my head. She asks, "Would you like to see me? Would you like to have a vision of me as you pass on to the next life?"

A long pause before I answer Mary. I've come to believe in these moments of shared imagination—when one's imagination is joined by the Holy. It's like a window that opens for a brief moment to the world of spirit that surrounds us. "Yes," I reply in my mind to Mary, "I'd love to see you as I die, but I don't want to die right now or anytime soon."

"Everyone dies, little one, but would you like to actually see me as you cross over?"

"Yes, I would love that."

"Then you will."

Now I'm thinking about my own dying but in a rather sweet way, as a transition to another existence. I'd love to have my two children with me at that time, and I wonder if my kindhearted, nonreligious son could see Mary too as I pass. Maybe he could begin to believe in a spiritual realm if he experienced a vision. I'm about to ask Mary if that could be possible when I hear her words.

"He will see me by the look on your face, Mary Ann."

I'm content. I can treasure this experience as an expression of love from the world beyond ordinary reality, but I can hold it lightly and not need to know if it will be literally true in the future. I turn back to this world, to the radio, with its banal but familiar holiday tunes.

A few moments later, as I wonder if I might write down this experience for my writer's critique group, I see in front of me—but really only in my mind—Mary, hovering halfway between sky and ground. No, this isn't an actual vision, and no, I'm not dying. But the shared imagination window swings open again just for an instant, and I see Mary with the most wonderful, broad smile on her face. She's beaming at me.

LETTERS TO JULIAN

Sometimes my imaginative conversations are with holy people rather than with God. One night, I was terribly upset about some issue, and I heard a voice in my mind say, "Perhaps I could help you."

I felt a bit freaked out, so I asked in my head, "Who are you?"

I heard back, "All shall be well, and all shall be well, and all manner of thing shall be well."

From my seminary years, I knew who that was, so I responded in my mind. "Hi, Julian. Thanks for that reassurance."

Julian of Norwich was an anchoress, living as a solitary nun in a small room attached to a church in Norwich, England, in the fourteenth century. She was well known as a spiritual director and was sought after for advice. One window of her cell opened into the church, through which she received Communion. The other window opened onto the road, through which she dispensed spiritual direction to those who sought her out. She had a near-death experience around the age of thirty, and at the urging of her priest, she wrote down the visions she saw during that experience. She went on to meditate on those visions and write down their deeper meanings during the rest of her life. Both the short and long versions of her writings are combined in a modern book called *Showings*.[59] This visionary woman began her mystical experience by graphically seeing Jesus suffer and die on the cross, and yet she wrote words of such great comfort and beauty. I love her.

That evening when Julian spoke to me in my mind, she seemed

---

[59] Edmund Colledge, OSA, and James Walsh, SJ, *Julian of Norwich: Showings* (New York: Paulist Press, 1978).

to suggest that I could talk to her whenever I needed comforting. She appeared to offer herself as a spiritual director to me, as she was to so many in her own time. Consequently, I actually go to the computer at times when I'm really stressed and write out questions to Julian. Then I wait and type out whatever comes to me as answers. I've been surprised at how helpful the responses are.

One of my trusted spiritual friends thinks that I'm simply writing what I know to be true in my deepest self. Perhaps that's accurate. I certainly don't need to believe that I'm dialoguing with a woman long dead! My best guess is that a deep part of myself is sharing with the Divine and imagining what that wise woman of the fourteenth century might say to me in the twenty-first century.

Most of my letters to Julian are about problems with other people—family members, friends, and others in the community. I guess I write to Julian because I can tell her the details and not divulge extremely private feelings to a living person. I'd still like to keep some turmoil private, but here are some of the comforting answers that have come from my imaginative letter writing with Julian.

One day, I asked Julian, "Can you tell me if I should feel bad about my outbursts today?"

This wise woman replied, "No, I can't tell you. You have to decide that. I can tell you that you are loved existentially here in the angelic realm and that they are proud of you for being honest and forceful. I am also proud of you, dear one. It took courage to say those things. It took control to get any sleep last night. It took self-preservation to speak out for yourself. Now, get some more sleep, and we can talk more in the morning."

On another occasion, I wrote, "How can I get through this time of extreme sadness?"

Julian answered, "Here are some ideas. I can't tell the details of the future, but I really can give suggestions on how to survive. You and I can plan and do some activities together that will ease your pain and get you through to better days. So here are some thoughts.

"Move. Do some kind of exercise daily.

"Rest. Take pills only at first, and sleep enough and at the same time every day.

"Pray. Start a regular time or times and pour your heart out to God, to Mary, to Sister Holy Spirit, and to me.

"Count. Count the good things in your life.

"Be assured. God is holding you especially securely during this time. You have only to see the God-incidences in the last several days. More are coming your way, Mary Ann. I have God's assurance on that. You are on his special hold-fast list right now until the time when things are better."

I asked, "When will things be better?"

"Any day now, things will start to look up. You'll see."

"Thanks, Julian. I love your encouraging words. I only wish I could really believe them."

"Wait and see, little one. It's getting lighter already."

"Is it?"

"Yes, I can see the new dawn for you, and it's just over the horizon. Hang on, sweet one, it will be here before you can blink twice."

"I just blinked twice. Is it here?"

"Well, no, not quite, but I thought you'd like a little levity. Have you ever tried laughing every day?"

"How?"

"I don't know. Rent funny movies. Think of funny times. Get your husband to tell you funny stories of his growing-up years. Anything will do. Just start laughing, and more laughter will come. It is contagious. Do you know the joke about the bishop who loved eating ice cream every day? One day he couldn't open the ice box, so he kicked it noisily downstairs. He had made an *ice screamer*."

"Not very good, Julian."

"Well, it's been a long time since I told a joke. I'll have a better one for you tomorrow."

"I look forward to that."

"Good. You need some bright things to look forward to."

My last example of corresponding with Julian actually ends with her most famous saying. I began with, "Could you please pray for me and my family? I'll pray, and I'll ask Mary to pray for us. I don't know any other power that can assist us, except divine help."

"Right, little one. Prayer is quite an energy, even though it seems puny on earth. It's the only force up here in heaven, and it's all-powerful. So, let go and let God, okay, sweetie?"

"I'll try. Thank you, Julian, for being here to help me when I need you. Thank our Lord for your help to me too. Here's an extra request. It may be too much to ask. But could God send me just a little sign that things are getting better? Just a little sign that I could recognize? That would be such a help tomorrow or the next day. Good night, Julian."

"Good night, sweet soul. All shall be well."

Although no sign from God showed up, I was comforted by my imaginary conversation with this wise spiritual director from the past. I treasure these experiences, knowing that such imaginings need to be pondered over time, savored, shared with trusted friends, and taken not as the literal utterances of God but as signposts on one's spiritual journey. However, I believe that sharing imagination through dreams and conversations with God and with holy people of the past can be enlightening, comforting, and spiritually trustworthy.

THE NEWCOMER'S TOUR

One evening I was devastated by problems with another person. I sat on the floor crying, wondering what to do. I needed to talk with someone. Julian? Sister Holy Spirit? Yes, I decided to chat with the Holy Spirit as if she were a female. Going to my computer, I began to write ideas that came to me in an imagined conversation with the third person of the Trinity. I pictured "her" coming toward me, then taking me by the hand.

She began with something reminiscent of a pickup line at a bar, "So, have you been here long?"

A bit dazed from crying and not quite knowing where I was in imagination, I stammered out, "Uh, I don't know."

Turning around with me, she gestured outward with her arm and continued, "Well, I think you have not been here much before now, so let's do the newcomer's guide, okay?"

"All right."

"So, do you know the first time I loved you?"

"No."

"It was the first time I looked upon you. You were a dear little thing, just born on the hospital gurney, even before your mother could be wheeled to the delivery room. A 'dirty baby,' they called you to your mother, and you couldn't be in the hospital nursery with the other infants."

"I remember my mom telling me that story, but I haven't felt angry about that until now. Now, I am a bit mad."

Chuckling, Sister Holy Spirit said, "Well, it's only right to feel angry at being excluded for bad reasons. You still get wounded at being excluded, don't you?"

"Yeah, if you mean feeling hurt that I was kicked out of that church's book course because I missed the first meeting, yes, it still upsets me."

"Well, my dear, here in heaven, it is quite the opposite. No one is ever excluded; all are welcomed with loving, open arms. Do you believe that? Do you feel that?"

Pessimistically, I replied, "I believe it, but at the moment, I don't feel it."

"Well, you will. Just stay with me, walk with me, and I'll show you. Now here's the delivery room, where new souls are born. Each one gets a big dose of God-love as they depart here."

"Cute."

"And here's where anguished souls sometimes come for rest and rebuilding. It's a tricky place to be in, because you don't want to stay here for too long, certainly not forever. But it's so necessary sometimes. This is almost an out-of-body place for souls. But we *love, love, love* them mightily while they are with us."

Sighing, I responded, "I wish I felt that."

"You will. Now here's the end of the soul's journey, when each one comes back to their native land of God. There's such joy here, beyond measure. We are all so glad to see the souls again. And they are always amazed at the love pouring toward them. You see, dying is so hard on earth that it seems like only pain to the departing. But once they get here, there is only joy—immeasurable amounts of it. Do you feel it, Mary Ann?"

"Not quite."

"Well, there are more rooms here. Let's keep to the tour. There's a special place I think you should see. It's for you and me to have a cup of tea or coffee together. Come on."

"Could we make it have a nice table and a pretty tablecloth and pretty china cups?" I asked, hopeful for the first time.

"Absolutely. And I think you would like light coming in through windows and a scene of nature visible through those windows, right? Anything else? How about the smell of chocolate and orange, and some Mozart or Mahler in the background, or an opera aria?"

"I'd love all those things. Thank you."

"Okay, here's the Mary Ann Room. Let's spend some time together here. What would you like right now, coffee or tea?"

"A flowery tea, please, and maybe a biscotti."

Serving me, Holy Spirit questioned, "Now talk to me, dear one. What's up to bring you here?"

"I'm so upset with this one person in my life. It seems I'm the only one who can feel right now, and I'm so tired of being the only one willing to talk about feelings. Can you help this person, maybe with a special angel who is expert in emotions and sharing?"

Sister Holy Spirit smiled. "Oh yes, we have specialist angels in that! We really do! And I'm feeling that this person could use some trust from *you* right now, correct?"

"Yes, but I can't trust right now."

"Well, you might try ..." she paused, thinking, "not to *pretend* ... but to *imagine*—that's it. *Imagine* that you can trust again. Then it can get easier and easier to *actually* trust."

"That sounds possible. Sounds good."

"Okay, moving forward, are there things you would like to do that would feel glorious?"

Thinking out loud, I rattled off a list. "Yes, I'd like to find just the right spiritual home in the city we've moved to, new friends, and things to do, including playing the flute professionally with orchestras. And I'd like a *grandchild*!"

Dusting off her hands, Holy Spirit replied, "Done. All done, in good time. Believe me."

"I do believe you."

"There now. Don't you feel better?"

Breathing a sigh, I replied, "Yes, actually I do."

"So, don't be a stranger here. Remember, there's a room here just for you and me to have tea and a chat. It's quite pretty, and you can come here anytime you want to. Just ask."

"I will." Reluctant to end the conversation, I continued, "Do you know my grandmothers?"

"Of course. Mary Addie and Lillie—and Mattie, if you count

great-grandmothers too. They look after you, you know. They're quite fond of you and think of you as being in a line of Celtic wise women."

"Well, please say hello and thank you to them for me."

"They say it right back to you too, Mary Ann. They do."

"I don't really want to leave this place in my imagination. It feels so safe. I don't want to go."

Like a patient teacher, Holy Spirit suggested, "Well, how about taking a nap in your world but also in this room that's made just for you and me? It could be quite restorative."

"That sounds wonderful. I'm going to nap as if I'm in both places. Thanks."

Bringing things to a close, Holy Spirit said with great love, "Thank *you* for coming and taking the tour. And thank you especially for writing about it. We are very real here, Mary Ann. Don't forget or doubt it. See you again. Have a great nap."

POETRY, PROSE, AND MUSIC

In the years since I first experienced shared imagination, I have had three moments when a creative idea came to me suddenly and whole, all at once. I don't consider myself a poet, or an author of fiction, or a composer. However, a poem, a short story, and a musical setting of a favorite prayer all came to me, at different times, but in a similar manner of a sudden download of information. Each time I remember feeling compelled to stand up, walk over to the computer or the piano, and start writing. I now think of these creative moments as offshoots of sharing imagination with the world of Spirit.

Although each entire work took only one sitting to write, the refashioning process took a good bit longer. Working on the poem involved many, many meetings with Grace Simpson, who at the time was the poet laureate of Virginia but also my soul friend and neighbor. Grace opened my eyes to the fun of refashioning a poem, of tweaking the words to provide better and better images and meanings. Grace also let me in on a writer's secret. "A poem is never finished," she told me. "At some point, you just stop working on it and let it stand." Here are the three creations I now let stand.

DESIGNS

I tugged until the white string broke in my hand,
      balled it up, tossed it away, then
             started again with another piece.

Around the chair legs,
      under the table, tangled
around the feet
          of the buffet,
everywhere, the cats
          had rolled a spool of thread.

They left behind a woven labyrinth
          of wild, reckless play.

And I, compulsive cleaner-upper,
          saw only a mess to banish
     until I stopped
          and read signs of *exuberant life*.

Does God, our Good Mother,
          take snapshots of our chaotic lines, our scattered
          endeavors whose patterns
          only She discerns and loves?
Does She tuck the photos in her scrapbook
to treasure,
          delighting in us even when we see no plan?

I resolve to believe so and to abandon myself,
    striding out in this direction,
        or that one
      or another
         wherever Shekinah* beckons,
    hoping the Weaver Herself might regard
      my haphazard cat's cradle
         and call it
Beautiful.

*In the Jewish and Christian traditions, the Shekinah is the feminine Divine Presence, literally *She Who Dwells With*

A TALE FOR ZEESHA

"Tomorrow you will be ridden by a stranger," said Zeesha's mother to him softly one night.

The little donkey stirred in his warm bed of straw near his mother, Seila, and replied, "I don't want a stranger to ride me, Mother! I have never carried anyone yet, and I am afraid of a stranger. Master has taken care of me since I was born. Let me be ridden only by him!"

"Sometimes, my little one, strangers can be kinder than our own masters. Let me tell you a story about your great-great-great-grandfather Lal and his master."

"Is it a good, long story, Mama? Long enough to let me stay awake late tonight, and good enough to make me drowsy with sleep when it is over?"

"You be the judge of that, little Zeesha. Here is the story: A long time ago in the nearby land of Moab, King Balak was facing war with the people of our own country, Israel. King Balak called for his prophet Balaam to curse the Israelites so that they might be defeated, and Balak and the Moabites become the victors. So, Balaam got up and saddled his donkey Lal, your ancestor, and set out for a hillside from which to overlook and curse the people of Israel.

"God's anger was kindled against Balaam because of his intention to bring harm, so God sent an angel to block the prophet's way upon the road. Not seeing the heavenly messenger, Balaam and two of his servants approached that spot. Suddenly, Lal saw the angel of the Lord with a drawn sword in his hand, and to protect his master, Lal veered off into the nearby field. Blind to the opposing angel, Balaam struck your poor ancestor Lal and forced him back onto the road.

"Next, the angel of the Lord stood in a narrow path between walled vineyards. There was very little space between those two walls, but Lal avoided the sword-bearing messenger by swerving to the right. Unfortunately, Lal scraped his own side and Balaam's foot painfully against the wall. Roaring with anger, Balaam struck poor Lal again.

"Then the Lord's angel went ahead and stood in an even narrower place, where there was no way to turn either to the right or to the left. When Lal perceived the angel in that narrowest of spots, he stopped in his tracks and lay down under Balaam. Angrier than ever, Balaam struck his donkey, this time with his heaviest staff.

"All at once, the Lord opened Lal's mouth, and the animal spoke aloud to his master, 'What have I done to you, that you have struck me these three times?'

"Balaam thundered back, 'I struck because you have made a fool of me three times! I wish I had a sword in my hand. I would kill you right now!'"

Seila paused in her story. "Imagine your ancestor's fear right then, my little one, his fear of his own master! But your forefather was brave and said to his master, 'Am I not your donkey, which you have ridden all your life to this day? Have I been in the habit of treating you this way?'

"His master reluctantly answered, 'No.'

"Suddenly, the Lord opened Balaam's eyes, and that Moabite prophet saw the angel, feet planted firmly on the path, his drawn sword in his hand. Balaam fell on his face in fear.

"The heavenly messenger said to Balaam, 'Why have you struck your donkey these three times? I have come out as an adversary, because your way is perverse before me. Your animal saw me and turned away from me these three times. If he had not turned away, surely just now I would have killed you and let your donkey live.'

"Then Balaam replied, 'I have sinned, for I did not know that you were standing in the path to oppose me. Now therefore, if it is pleasing to you, I will return home.'

"The angel countered, 'No, you must go to this Moabite king, but speak only what I tell you.'"

Seila interrupted her tale to look right at her colt. "Know this, my little one. Your forefather, Lal's master, did as he was told and overlooked the camp of the Israelites and prophesied blessings for them. Then he foretold that a great star, a king, would come from the people of Israel. These were Balaam's prophetic words.

'I see him, but not now;
I behold him, but not near—
A star shall come out of Jacob
And a scepter shall rise out of Israel.'

"So you see, my little Zeesha, masters do not always make the best riders for us."

"I see, Mama, but who is this stranger who will ride me tomorrow? Will he be kind?"

"He is a kind, gentle, good man, Zeesha, a healer. He is also the king whom Balaam foresaw so long ago."

"A king! I shall carry a king? Yes, I will let him ride me! Imagine, Mother, I will be the greatest in our family. For who among all our kin has ever been ridden by royalty?"

"Well, my proud one, I myself have carried a queen many years ago, before you were born."

"A queen! You never told me that story, Mother. Tell me that one now, for your first story has not taken up enough of the night's passing, and it has most certainly not made me drowsy enough for sleep. Tell me about the queen, Mama, tell me!"

"She would later be called the queen of heaven, my little one, but on that journey, she was a simple maid, very great with child, who needed me to give her some rest on her journey to Bethlehem. Her husband, Joseph, had to travel to that city on man's business, but I knew that I was carrying the young woman to Bethlehem on God's business."

"How did you know, Mother?"

"Angels still appear to us, Zeesha, just as they did to your ancestor. It is often hard to make men understand what we have seen, though sometimes a few people will seem to comprehend, like Mary, the young maid who rode me to Bethlehem." Gazing pensively at the stars, the older, graying animal spoke softly. "You know, I sometimes think that perhaps humans do see and hear angels at times, only not quite as clearly as we donkeys do. At any rate, after I carried that poor, weary maiden to Bethlehem, she and Joseph stayed with me and the other animals in a stable while the young woman gave birth to her firstborn child, a son. There was a great star that night, Zeesha, a star like the one our ancestor's master prophesied about. And there were angels all over the sky, little one. I heard from their song that Mary's son is indeed a king, the Son of the Most High God. And he will be the one who will ride you tomorrow into Jerusalem."

"Will I be famous, Mama? Will the king be great, and live in the palace, and bring me and you and all our family to live in a grand stable?" Will he, Mother, will he?"

"No, my child, although the crowds will cheer him and wave palm branches for him, I am afraid that the angels have said that he will soon be arrested and executed. He will die not long after you carry him to the city."

"Then I shall not take him! If he is as good as you say, and kind, and a king, and the Son of the Most High, then I will not carry him to his death!"

"Sometimes we must carry the Word of God to a place of birth, and sometimes we must carry it into a dark time, a time even of death, Zeesha. But do not be afraid; the angels have whispered to me of a great hope. A great miracle is waiting, my stubborn one, and we must do our part and wait with hope."

"What miracle, Mama, what great hope?"

"I know only that we must be on a certain hillside one day soon, near dawn, and we shall see that star which your forefather's master foretold. We shall see that star rise again in a new way. We shall be together, waiting patiently near a garden to see the angels' promise come true. I think we shall laugh and leap for joy together on that hillside, my dear one. Would you like that?"

But Zeesha had finally succumbed to sleep, nestled near the older donkey's flank.

Seila, pondering these things in her heart, spoke into the darkness. "You see, my young one, sometimes we are called to resist evil, sometimes to carry to new birth, and sometimes to travel to the valley of the shadow of death. And sometimes we must simply wait in the dark for hope to arise like a star. But if we listen to the angels whispering to us, then we can take our small part in God's great plans. Tomorrow you will carry a stranger."

AN EVENING PRAYER⁶⁰

M. A. Archer

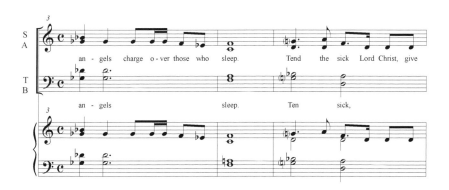

---

⁶⁰ *The Book of Common Prayer, according to the use of The Episcopal Church* (The Church Hymnal Corporation and Seabury Press, 1977), 134.

Copyright Mary Ann Archer, 2012

CONCLUSION

THE COSMIC EQUATION

Thank you for traveling with me on this journey through moments of shared imagination, time spent imagining with the Holy, with other people, and over time. I hope something in you resonated with my own and others' stories

I would love to help others form and run the three-part group format that Pamela has invented and guided—meditation, conversation, and evening prayer—where shared imagination can be practiced. My hope is that the accounts I've written in this book will garner interest in hearing more about this potentially life-changing way of encountering God. What might result from that interest—workshops, lectures, another book? I count on God to help us imagine that.

There is a passage in Ephesians that sums up for me not only our *ability* to imagine with the Divine but also our *invitation* to do that imagining.

Ephesians 3:20 says: "Glory to God, whose power working within us can do infinitely more than we can ask or imagine."[61]

I have nicknamed this verse "The Cosmic Equation," although, strictly speaking, it is an *inequality*, a "more than" mathematical construct. It might look like this in a math book:

$$\textit{God's workings} \;\infty \gg \textit{our asking and imagining}$$

---

[61] *The Book of Common Prayer, according to the use of The Episcopal Church* (The Church Hymnal Corporation and Seabury Press, 1977), 102.

Our part of the inequality is to *ask* and *imagine*; God's part is to infinitely surpass what we request and conjure up in imagination. Isn't that beautiful, invitational, and stuffed full of hope? God wants us to petition and visualize, and in return, God promises to do *infinitely* more than we can envision! So, I leave you with Pamela's gentle conditions and God's invitation. "While testing the fruits and checking with trusted others, *come imagine with the Holy!*" Our infinitely generous God is waiting to share imagination with you.

ACKNOWLEDGMENTS

First and foremost, I must thank my dear friend Pamela Barnett, who introduced me to the Ignatian-styled, imaginative meditating process, which inspired me to write this book. Pamela and I met at our church in northern New Jersey in the late 1970s and quickly became fast friends. This wise woman opened for me new depths of beauty, especially concerning home decorating and fine art. Most importantly for this book, she introduced me to the real possibility of connecting with the Divine in everyday life. In midlife, Pamela moved from our prosperous New Jersey suburb of New York City to faraway Rapid City, South Dakota, near the Black Hills—a site holy to Native Americans. When asked why she moved to such a seemingly remote area, she would simply answer, "Because God is here." Sadly, she passed away several years ago, but now she is surely even more where God is.

I owe a great debt also to Margaret Guenther, whose book *Holy Listening* propelled me to become a spiritual director. As head of the Center for Christian Spirituality at General Theological Seminary, she interviewed me for entrance there, encouraging me to dive into all that the seminary offered. I treasured her wonderful lectures at the center because of her wisdom, practicality, and humor. Although Margaret passed away as I was working on this book, I did speak with her by phone about the work shortly before her death and received wise answers, encouragement, and spry good humor.

I'd like to thank all the people who shared their stories with me and gave me permission to include their accounts here. Their names and life details have been altered, or not, according to their wishes. Their tales still inspire me.

I also thank author and teacher Margaret Bigger for editing my writing and constantly cheering me on in the process. She introduced me to the unexpected joy of rewriting, organizing, and rewording.

My thanks also go to four more people who agreed to read and edit my manuscript: Sarah Norton, editor of *The Rose in the World*; Anne Silver, author of *Trustworthy Connections: Interpersonal Issues in Spiritual Direction*; Rob Mikulak, a gifted professional editor; and Sandie Akers, a dear and trustworthy spiritual friend.

Most importantly, I must thank my sweet, supportive husband, Frank, who has believed in me in this work and in all my endeavors.

APPENDIX A

AIDS FOR MEETINGS

Starting a Shared Imagination Group

If you are a layperson, as I am, speak with your clergy about your desire to start this type of gathering. Both lay persons and clergy wishing to start a group might want to explain the imaginative method and the three-part meeting format at a vestry meeting or similar church assembly. The meetings should last ninety minutes to two hours. I call my current group "Imagining with Scripture." Pamela called our first gatherings "The Women's Spiritual Direction Group." Choose a name you feel comfortable with that best describes the meetings to prospective members.

Choose a meeting room. These gatherings work best in something like a church parlor, with comfortable, upholstered furniture, eye-level lighting, and a door that can be closed—for confidentiality. I've had to politely but firmly insist on those requirements when offered a classroom with hard chairs, desks, and overhead lights or an open space with upholstered seating but no door!

When and how often should the group gather? I don't have a definitive answer for that question. When Pamela Barnett formed our very first circle, we met every Monday night for about six years! After those first years, Pamela decided the group would gather weekly for three eight-week sessions, starting in the fall and taking breaks during Advent and Lent. Currently, I'm holding meetings on the second and fourth Sundays, 4:00–5:30 evenings for five or six meetings, again with breaks for Advent and Lent. My best advice to readers of this book is to get started in any format and adapt as you go along.

To publicize the group, ask if you or a clergy person can make an announcement at a church service about this new gathering. Have the group's description and meeting dates announced in print in Sunday service bulletins and in monthly or weekly church newsletters. Most importantly, speak directly with women about your own excitement at encountering God through this imagination-filled method. A face-to-face conversation is the common denominator that propelled *all* the women in my various groups to join.

In Advent and sometimes in Lent or midsummer, I like to schedule a longer meeting of a half-day "Quiet Morning" or "Quiet Afternoon." Imagination in meditation is always the center point of these longer gatherings, but I often enlist other people to read the beginning and ending prayers, help make artistic name tags, or run a short art project. Sometimes I ask a clergy person to join the gathering and lead a short communion service. Half-day meetings are a wonderful way to get more folks, including men, experiencing active imagination in meditation. For these gatherings, I provide a typed handout containing the focus of the day's meditation and four suggested ways to spend the quiet time—based on the four Myers-Briggs temperaments discussed at length in the book *Prayer and Temperament: Different Prayer Forms for Different Personality Types* by Michael and Norrisey. (See my reference to this text in Appendix B: Meditation Topics.) I use the following thumbnail sketch of each temperament's preferred meditation path: SJs like to go back in time to become part of a Bible scene. NSs prefer to bring that story forward and imagine encountering the characters (divine and human) in the present. NTs often enjoy making a list of the virtues found in a story. SPs are free spirits who pray while doing some activity and can encounter the Holy One while helping the group leader set up for the luncheon to come or by taking a walk outside and observing God through the natural world. I invite you to read the Michael/Norrisey book for a fuller description of the temperaments and their prayer preferences.

Running a Group Meeting

Before participants arrive at the chosen room, arrange the seating in a roughly circular form. I like to claim a tall-backed wing chair in the circle for my own seat, to visually announce that I'm acting as the facilitator/shepherdess—a non-clergy leader with overtones of spiritual friendship.

Set out on a central, low table: a candle (I use battery-powered ones for safety these days), colored index cards, pens, and a book—any book. The candle will be lit during meditation. The index cards are for people to write down their prayer requests. The book is where they stick their written requests.

As the members arrive, invite them to write out their own prayer requests for themselves, friends, and relatives, the community, the nation, or the world. Participants can write the first name of people for whom they are praying, or they can write a nonspecific request such as—"for a person recently diagnosed with cancer." Specifically invite people to pray for themselves, since we often feel we may only pray for the needs of others. Prayers of thanksgiving and gratitude are also encouraged. When the participants have written their prayers, invite them to stick the cards into the book on the table. Explain that you will pass these prayers out during the closing prayer service and have each person read the prayers aloud as we go around the circle. If a person receives her or his own prayer card, he or she may trade with their neighbor. Encourage individuals to keep the prayer card they've received and to pray for those concerns as often as they feel called to during the time until the next meeting.

When the meetings are first formed and when *any new person comes to the gathering*, pass out the handout on meditating and discussion guidelines found later in this chapter. Have each person read aloud a paragraph or so of this handout, going around the circle. Those who would rather not read can pass to the next person. Poor eyesight, poor reading ability, or preference for another language (often Spanish) can make a person uncomfortable reading out loud in a group. Make sure each individual knows that everything is gentle and invitational in this circle, and that even reading aloud is *not* required.

Go around the circle again, having each member introduce herself or himself and possibly share other details—profession, passions, children, spouse or partner, years in that city or in that church. Make sure the participants know that this sharing is voluntary—the only requirement is to give one's first name. Members may also "check in," describing briefly how they are feeling or what's happening in their lives right now.

After writing prayer requests, going over guidelines, and self-introductions, begin the meditation portion of the gathering. Ask the participants to find a comfortable position in their chair or on their sofa and invite them to close their eyes. Read aloud the Relaxation Talk found later in this appendix. Once the circle has relaxed and breathed in God, read out loud the passage of scripture or book upon which the group will meditate, suggesting ways to enter the story or passage. Make sure to encourage folks to go elsewhere in meditation if they feel so called during the quiet time.

While the group is in silence, I like to briefly meditate myself, always keeping one part of my brain aware of the time passing. I usually ask God and my inner clock when to bring the gathering out of meditation. The sentence I use is, "And when you're ready, either now or in a few moments, I invite you to wrap up your conversation or experience, open your eyes, and become present in this room again."

I look around at the group, then gently ask, "How did that time go for any of you?" At that point, I stare at the rug and *wait*. That empty time can feel awkward, but usually someone speaks up, and the sharing time begins. I always comfort myself during those first few silent moments with my firm belief that even if no one shares, the group can wrap up the meeting with the closing prayer and still know that God has been working among us.

As an individual shares what came up during the silence, I try to gently tease out more details of the imaginative encounter. I might ask questions like "How did that feel?" "What did Jesus's look or words seem to mean?" "What else came up?" I try to model for the others in the circle the nondirective questions that are best for the discussion portion of the meeting. We may suggest what another person's image might mean to us or say what has helped us in a similar life circumstance. However, just asking questions for more details and expressing joy or wonder at what has bubbled up for another person is the best, most affirming way of responding to each member's sharing.

When it seems that each individual who wants to speak has shared, I open the floor for "Last Comments." During this time, a person may add *anything* (except politics!) to the group's conversation. Last Comments is my own addition to the meeting format, and I've found it fascinating and fun to see what folks may bring up during this time. This interval is usually short, since most people have shared rather completely already. However, interesting ideas often pop up and can be briefly discussed before moving on to the closing prayer portion of the gathering.

To end the meeting, I hand out the Compline/Closing Prayer Service, printed later in this appendix, which I've crafted from three sources—the Episcopal *Book of Common Prayer,* the Presbyterian *Book of Common Worship,* and the Anglican *New Zealand Book of Prayer.*

The group reads through the service aloud, and I pick out one psalm, one prayer from the numbered prayers, one form of the Lord's Prayer, and one closing prayer as we go along. At the time for intercessions, I hand out the prayer cards written at the beginning of the meeting and have each member read the one she or he has received. Going back to the Closing Prayer Service, we continue with the last sections—prayers, the Song of Simeon, and the closing words. I thank each member for showing up that evening and remind the gathering of the date of the next meeting.

That's it. That's how I run a meeting. Following these steps, you too can lead a gathering of shared imagination!

Imagining in One-on-One Sessions

Whenever I meet individually for the first time with a directee, I explain that I'm comfortable with two modes of operating—(1) the client talks, and I listen, making some gentle, intuitive comments or questions, or (2) I guide the directee into a short session of imagining in meditation, and we discuss what came up during the silence. I let the directee choose which method he or she would like to use. Often, we end up employing a bit of both methods. During a session, when I feel the time might be right for meditation, I often suggest a brief time of envisioning. Again, I always let my guest decide if meditating seems right for the moment.

The process is exactly the same as in a group setting. I use the same relaxation talk, suggest a topic/scene/story, and invite my client to go where the Spirit leads. I find I can let myself imagine while my directee is in silence, keeping part of my brain aware of how much time is passing. If any of my meditative ideas seem useful to my client, I *may* relate them but only after the directee has fully explored his or her own meditation, and only if my thoughts won't leave my head unless I speak them.

I've even used this method when doing a phone session with a client! It may feel silly to go into silence while talking on the phone, but I've found that the quiet period is always charged with God-energy. The envisioning images are just as vivid even when the directee and I are hundreds of miles distant from each other, not because of any skill on our part but because God is incredibly generous with imagination!

THE RELAXATION TALK

Find a comfortable spot in the chair or on the sofa, with your hands open and receptive and your feet resting easily on the floor. With your eyes closed, begin to scan your body for any tension, tightness or dis-ease. Beginning at your feet, flex and relax the muscles in your toes, the arches of your feet, your ankles. Let go of any tightness in the calves of your legs; relax any tension in your thighs and let your stomach muscles just go slack. Begin to take in a few deep breaths, and as you inhale, breathe in God's light and love, God's strength and healing power. As you breathe out, imagine surrounding yourself with that light, love, and healing power, much as the candle flame on our table is surrounded by light and heat.

Feel the chair or sofa supporting your back. Relax the muscles in your shoulders. Release any tension in the muscles of your upper arms, your lower arms, your palms, and fingers. Feel any tightness flowing out the tips of your fingers. Again, breathe in God's light, love, strength, and healing power. Breathe out all things that seem heavy or burdensome. Hand over to God all cares, worries, and responsibilities, things that need to be done and things we wish we had not done. Let God hold all those things during these moments, so that we don't have to.

Let go of any tension in your neck and jaw. Release any tightness around your mouth and around your eyes. Imagine you can even relax behind your eyes. Let your forehead smooth out and picture all the rest of the tension in your body flowing out the top of your head. One more time, breathe in God's light, unconditional love, and power to heal whatever needs healing in you right now. As you exhale, breathe out the things of yesterday, today, and tomorrow, so that we might meet God in God's eternal now, where only these moments matter.

HANDOUTS

Make printed copies of the following for your meetings.

Meditating

There is no wrong way to meditate! During contemplation, we may see images and hear words, or think thoughts, or go with our distractions—which are often the Holy Spirit calling us to something important. Some of us may simply sit quietly in the presence of God. A person may experience different types of imaginings at different meetings. A few of us may even fall asleep on occasion. God brings us what we need at the time—even if that is much-needed rest. We need to reassure ourselves that there is no wrong way to spend the quiet period and that whatever comes is God's gift to us for this meeting.

ASSISTS and Holy Forgetting[62]

Ask gentle questions.
Skip the
Shoulds.
I
Statements.
Time for
Silence.

---

[62] Margaret Guenther, *Holy Listening: The Art of Spiritual Direction* (Cambridge, MA: Cowley Publications, 1992), 30, 19.

These guidelines for discussion encourage gentleness with each other as we talk "across the circle." We may ask open-ended questions for clarification about what a person has revealed of his or her thoughts, faith, or life. We can ask questions such as, "Could God be asking or leading you to do this or that?" We avoid all statements such as "you should," "you will," or "you ought to." As we hear another's comments, each of us is free to decide if those ideas resonate with our experience or not, accepting those ideas as helpful or setting them aside.

Another model for our group work is to stick mostly to "I statements." In other words, we can say things like, "I feel this way," or "I have experienced this in a similar situation." We may gently offer our ideas on another person's meditational images and experiences, but always owning them as our projections or interpretations that may or may not resonate with the meditating person.

Silence is also an important part of our discussions together. God often needs our silence to speak to us. The other members of the circle may also need our silence to share with the group. Extroverts sometimes begin talking after four or five seconds of silence, while introverts might wait seven to ten seconds before they speak up. We may all need to wait a few uncomfortable moments before we jump in and talk. We may also need to limit how many times we speak up. If we find ourselves commenting after every person has shared his or her quiet time experience, it is time to refrain from speaking for a while. Studying the pattern on a rug, pillow, or picture is a good way to pass the waiting-in-silence time. Even if no one speaks up, we can say our closing prayer, go home, and know that God has still been working among us.

All our conversations must also be treated with *strict confidentiality* as we practice what author Margaret Guenther calls "Holy Forgetting." Everything that is said in this room stays in this room, with one exception. Sharing our own experiences with people outside the gathering is within the guidelines and may help a new person decide to come and try our group process for themselves. However, all the other members' words must stay in this room.

Using these guidelines can help us create an atmosphere of gentleness and trust, where we can safely bring up our sensitive, troubled, or joyful thoughts and experiences. Practicing this "assists" method and "Holy Forgetting," each one of us assists in the process of discerning where God may be leading us.

Compline: Prayer at the Close of Day
from the Episcopal *Book of Common Prayer*[63]
the Presbyterian *Book of Common Worship*[64]

Opening Sentences

The Lord Almighty grant us a peaceful night and a perfect end. *Amen.*

Our help is in the Name of the Lord;
The maker of heaven and earth.

Prayer of Confession

Almighty God, Maker of all things,
Have mercy on us.
Jesus Christ, Redeemer of the world,
Have mercy on us.
Holy Spirit, giver of life,
Have mercy on us.

Merciful God,
we confess that we have sinned against you
in thought, word, and deed,
by what we have done,
and by what we have left undone.
We have not loved you
with our whole heart and mind and strength;
we have not loved our neighbors as ourselves.
In your mercy forgive what we have been,
help us amend what we are,
and direct what we shall be,
so that we may delight in your will

---

[63] *The Book of Common Prayer, according to the use of The Episcopal Church* (The Church Hymnal Corporation and Seabury Press, 1977), 127–135.
[64] *Book of Common Worship* (Louisville, KY: John Knox Press, 1993), 551–561.

and walk in your ways,
to the glory of your holy name.
Amen.

Psalm (Author's note: for beautiful and *inclusive* language Psalms, try the *St. Helena Psalter*.[65])

Psalm 4
Answer me when I call, O God, defender of my cause;*
      you set me free when I am hard-pressed;
      have mercy on me and hear my prayer.

"You mortals, how long will you dishonor my glory;*
      how long will you worship dumb idols and run after false gods?"

Know that the LORD does wonders for the faithful;*
      when I call upon the LORD, will hear me.

Tremble, then, and do not sin;*
      speak to your heart in silence upon your bed.

Offer the appointed sacrifices,*
      and put your trust in the LORD.

Many are saying, "Oh, that we might see better times!"*
      Lift up the light of your countenance upon us, O LORD.

You have put gladness in my heart,*
      more than when grain and wine and oil increase.

I lie down in peace; at once I fall asleep;*
      for only you, LORD, make me dwell in safety.

Psalm 23
The LORD is my shepherd;*

---

[65] The Order of St. Helena, *The Saint Helena Psalter* (NY: Church Publishing Incorporated, 2004).

I shall not be in want.
He makes me lie down in green pastures*
  and leads me beside still waters.

He revives my soul*
  and guides me along right pathways for his Name's sake.

Though I walk through the valley of the shadow of death,
I shall fear no evil,*
  for you are with me; your rod and your staff, they comfort me.

You spread a table before me in the presence of those who trouble me;*
  you have anointed my head with oil, and my cup is running over.

Surely your goodness and mercy shall follow me
all the days of my life,*
  and I will dwell in the house of the LORD for ever.

Psalm 31
In you, O LORD, have I taken refuge; let me never be put to shame;*
  deliver me in your righteousness.

Incline your ear to me;*
  make haste to deliver me.

Be my strong rock, a castle to keep me safe,
for you are my crag and my stronghold;*
for the sake of your Name, lead me and guide me.

Take me out of the net that they have secretly set for me,*
  for you are my tower of strength.

Into your hands I commend my spirit,*
  for you have redeemed me, O LORD, O God of truth.

Psalm 33

Rejoice in the LORD, you righteous;*
	it is good for the just to sing praises.

Praise the LORD with the harp;*
	play upon the psaltery and lyre.

Sing for him a new song;*
	sound a fanfare with all your skill upon the trumpet.

For the word of the LORD is right,*
	and all his works are sure.

He loves righteousness and justice;*
	the loving-kindness of the LORD fills the whole earth.

Our soul waits for the LORD;*
	he is our help and our shield.
Indeed, our heart rejoices in him,*
	for in his holy Name we put our trust.

Let your loving-kindness, O LORD, be upon us,*
	as we have put our trust in you.

Psalm 34

I will bless the LORD at all times,*
	his praise shall ever be in my mouth.

I will glory in the LORD;*
	let the humble hear and rejoice.

Proclaim with me the greatness of the LORD;*
	let us exalt his Name together.

I sought the LORD, and he answered me*
	and delivered me out of all my terror.

Look upon him and be radiant,*
> and let not your faces be ashamed.

I called in my affliction, and the LORD heard me*
> and saved me from all my troubles.

The angels of the LORD encompass those who fear him,*
> and he will deliver them.

Taste and see that the LORD is good;*
> happy are they who trust in him!

Psalm 91
He who dwells in the shelter of the Most High*
> abide under the shadow of the Almighty.

He shall say to the LORD, "You are my refuge and my stronghold,*
> my God in whom I put my trust."

He shall deliver you from the snare of the hunter*
> and from the deadly pestilence.

He shall cover you with his pinions, and you shall find refuge under
his wings;*
> his faithfulness shall be a shield and buckler.

You shall not be afraid of any terror by night*
> nor of the arrow that flies by day;

Of the plague that stalks in the darkness*
> nor of the sickness that lays waste at mid-day.

A thousand shall fall at your side and ten thousand at your right hand,*
> but it shall not come near you.

Your eyes have only to behold,*

to see the reward of the wicked.

Because you have made the LORD your refuge*
    and the Most High your habitation,

There shall no evil happen to you,*
    neither shall any plague come near your dwelling.

For he shall give his angels charge over you,*
    to keep you in all your ways.

They shall bear you in their hands,*
    lest you dash your foot against a stone.

You shall tread upon the lion and adder;*
    you shall trample the young lion and the serpent under your feet.

Because he is bound to me in love, therefore will I deliver him;*
    I will protect him, because he knows my Name.

He shall call upon me, and I will answer him;*
    I am with him in trouble; I will rescue him and bring him honor.

With long life will I satisfy him*
    and show him my salvation.

Psalm 121
I lift up my eyes to the hills;*
    from where is my help to come?

My help comes from the LORD,*
    the maker of heaven and earth.

He will not let your foot be moved;*
    And he who watches over you will not fall asleep.

Behold, he who keeps watch over Israel*
      shall neither slumber nor sleep;

The LORD himself watches over you*
      The LORD is your shade at your right hand,

So that the sun shall not strike you by day,*
      nor the moon by night.

The LORD shall preserve you from all evil,*
      it is he who shall keep you safe.

The LORD shall watch over your going out and your coming in,*
      from this time forth for evermore.

Psalm 126
When the LORD restored the fortunes of Zion,*
      then were we like those who dream.

Then was our mouth filled with laughter,*
      and our tongue with shouts of joy.

Then they said among the nations,*
      "The LORD has done great things for them."

The LORD has done great things for us,*
      and we are glad indeed.

Restore our fortunes, O LORD,*
      like the watercourses of the Negev.

Those who sowed with tears*
      will reap with songs of joy,

Those who go out weeping, carrying the seed,*
      will come again with joy, shouldering their sheaves.

Psalm 131
O LORD, I am not proud;*
      I have no haughty looks.

I do not occupy myself with great matters,*
      or with things that are too hard for me.

But I still my soul and make it quiet,
      like a child upon its mother's breast;*
      my soul is quieted within me.

O Israel, wait upon the LORD,*
      from this time forth for evermore.

Psalm 134
Behold now, bless the LORD, all you servants of the LORD,*
      you that stand by night in the house of the LORD.

Lift up your hands in the holy place and bless the LORD;*
      the LORD who made heaven and earth bless you out of Zion.

Psalm 139
LORD, you have searched me out and known me;*
      you know my sitting down and my rising up;
      you discern my thoughts from afar.

You trace my journeys and my resting places,*
      and are acquainted with all my ways.

Indeed, there is not a word on my lips,*
      but you, O LORD, know it altogether.

You press upon me behind and before,*
      and lay your hand upon me.

Such knowledge is too wonderful for me;*
      it is so high that I cannot attain to it.

Where can I go then from your spirit;*
>   where can I flee from your presence?

If I climb up to heaven, you are there;*
>   if I make the grave my bed, you are there also.

If I take the wings of the morning*
>   and dwell in the uttermost parts of the sea,

Even there your hand will lead me,*
>   and your right hand hold me fast.

If I say, "Surely the darkness will cover me,*
>   and the light around me turn to night."

Darkness is not dark to you; the night is as bright as the day;*
>   darkness and light to you are both alike.

For you yourself created my inmost parts;*
>   you knit me together in my mother's womb.

I will thank you because I am marvelously made;*
>   your works are wonderful, and I know it well.

My body was not hidden from you,*
>   while I was being made in secret
>   and woven in the depths of the earth.

Your eyes beheld my limbs, yet unfinished in the womb;*
>   all of them were written in your book;*
>   they were fashioned day by day,
>   when as yet there was none of them.

How deep I find your thoughts, O God;*
>   how great is the sum of them!

If I were to count them, they would be more in number than the sand;*
　　to count them all, my life span would need to be like yours.

Search me out, O God, and know my heart;*
　　try me and know my restless thoughts.

Look well whether there be any wickedness in me,*
　　and lead me in the way that is everlasting.

(Following the Psalm …)

Glory to the Father and to the Son, and to the Holy Spirit:
As it was in the beginning, is now, and will be for ever. Amen.

Scripture Reading

(One of the following is read.)

> Come to me, all you that are weary and are carrying heavy burdens, and I will give you rest. Take my yoke upon you, and learn from me; for I am gentle and humble in heart, and you will find rest for your souls. For my yoke is easy, and my burden is light. (Matt. 11:28–30)
>
> May the God of peace… sanctify you entirely; and may your spirit and soul and body be kept sound and blameless at the coming of our Lord Jesus Christ. (1 Thess. 5:23)
>
> It is the God who said, "Let light shine out of darkness," who has shone in our hearts to give the light of the knowledge of the glory of God in the face of Jesus Christ. (2 Cor. 4:6–10)
>
> Peace I leave with you; my peace I give to you. I do not give to you as the world gives. Do not let your hearts be troubled, and do not let them be afraid. (John 14:272)

I am convinced that neither death, nor life, nor angels, nor rulers, nor things present, nor things to come, nor powers, nor height, nor depth, nor anything else in all creation, will be able to separate us from the love of God in Christ Jesus our Lord. (Rom. 8:38–39)

Hear, O Israel: The Lord is our God, the Lord alone. You shall love the Lord your God with all your heart, and with all your soul, and with all your might. Keep these words that I am commanding you today in your heart. Recite them to your children and talk about them when you are at home and when you are away, when you lie down and when you rise. (Deut. 6:4–7)

The word of the Lord
Thanks be to God.

Prayer

Into your hand, O Lord, I commend my spirit;
For you have redeemed me, O Lord, O God of truth.
Keep us, O Lord, as the apple of your eye;
Hide us under the shadow of your wings.
In righteousness I shall see you;
When I awake your presence shall give me joy.
I will lie down in peace and take my rest,
For in God alone I dwell unafraid.

(One of the following versions of the Lord's Prayer is said.)

Our Father, who art in heaven,
hallowed be thy Name,
thy kingdom come,
thy will be done,
on earth as it is in heaven.
Give us this day our daily bread.
And forgive us our debts,

as we forgive our debtors.
And lead us not into temptation,
but deliver us from evil.
For thine is the kingdom,
and the power, and the glory,
forever.
Amen.

Or

Our Father in heaven,
hallowed be your Name,
your kingdom come,
your will be done,
on earth as in heaven.
Give us today our daily bread.
Forgive us our sins, as we forgive
those who sin against us.
Save us from the time of trial,
and deliver us from evil.
For the kingdom, the power,
and the glory are yours
now and forever. Amen.

Or

Eternal Spirit,
Earth-maker, Pain-bearer, Life-giver,
Source of all that is and that shall be,
Father and Mother of us all,
Loving God, in whom is heaven:

The hallowing of your name echo through the universe!
The way of your justice be followed by the peoples
of the world!
Your heavenly will be done by all created beings!

Your commonwealth of peace and freedom
sustain our hope and come on earth.

With the bread we need for today, feed us,
In the hurts we absorb from one another, forgive us,
In times of temptation and test, strengthen us.
From trials too great to endure, spare us.
From the grip of all that is evil, free us.

For you reign in the glory of the power that is love,
now and for ever. Amen.[66]
(Used by permission: *A New Zealand Prayer
Book—He Karakia Mihinare o Aotearoa*)

(One of the following prayers is then said.)

1.

O Lord, support us all the day long
until the shadows lengthen
and the evening comes,
and the busy world is hushed,
and the fever of life is over,
and our work is done.
Then, in your mercy,
grant us a safe lodging,
and a holy rest,
and peace at the last;
through Jesus Christ our Lord.
Amen.

2.

O God, you have designed this wonderful world,

---

[66] The Anglican Church in Aotearoa, New Zealand, and Polynesia, *A New
Zealand Prayer Book—He Karakia Mihinare o Aotearoa* (San Francisco, California:
HarperSanFrancisco, 1989), 181.

and know all things good for us.
Give us such faith
that, by day and by night,
at all times and in all places,
we may without fear
entrust those who are dear to us
to your never-failing love,
in this life
and in the life to come;
through Jesus Christ our Lord.
Amen.

3.

O God, who appointed the day for labor
and the night for rest:
Grant that we may rest in peace and quietness
during the coming night
so that tomorrow
we may go forth to our appointed labors.
Take us into your holy keeping,
that no evil may befall us
nor any ill come near our home.
When at last our days are ended
and our work is finished,
grant that we may depart in your peace,
in the sure hope of that glorious kingdom
where there is day without night,
light without darkness,
and life without shadow of death forever;
through Jesus Christ,
the Light of the world.
Amen.

4.

Visit this place, O Lord,
and drive from it all snares of the enemy;

let your holy angels dwell with us
to preserve us in peace;
and let your blessing be upon as always,
through Jesus Christ our Lord.
Amen.

5.

Send your peace into our hearts, O Lord,
at the evening hour,
that we may be contented with your mercies of this day,
and confident of your protection for this night;
and now, having forgiven others,
even as you forgive us,
may we have a pure comfort
and a healthful rest
within the shelter of our homes;
through Jesus Christ our Savior.
Amen.

6.

Be our light in the darkness, O Lord,
and in your great mercy
defend us from all perils and dangers of this night;
for the love of your only son,
our Savior Jesus Christ.
Amen.

7.

Be present, merciful God,
and protect us through the silent hours of this night,
so that we who are wearied
by the changes and chances of this fleeting world
may rest in your eternal changelessness;
through Jesus Christ our Lord.
Amen.

(One of the following prayers may be added.)

1.

Keep watch, dear Lord,
With those who work or watch
or weep this night,
and give your angels charge over those who sleep.
Tend the sick, Lord Christ;
give rest to the weary,
bless the dying,
soothe the suffering,
pity the afflicted,
shield the joyous;
and all for your love's sake.
Amen.

2.

O God,
your unfailing providence
sustains the world we live in
and the life we live:
Watch over those, both night and day,
who work while others sleep,
and grant that we may never forget
that our common life depends
upon each other's toil;
through Jesus Christ our Lord.
Amen.

(Silence may be kept, and free intercessions and thanksgivings may be offered.)

Canticle of Simeon

Refrain: Guide us waking O Lord,
and guard us sleeping;
that awake we may watch with Christ,
and asleep we may rest in peace.

Lord, you now have set your servant free
to go in peace as you have promised,

For these eyes of mine have seen the Savior,
whom you have prepared for all the world to see:

A Light to enlighten the nations,
and the glory of your people Israel.

Glory to the Father, and to the Son, and to the Holy Spirit;
As it was in the beginning, is now, and will be for ever. Amen.

Refrain: Guide us waking, O Lord,
and guard us sleeping;
that awake we may watch with Christ,
and asleep we may rest in peace.

Dismissal

Let us bless the Lord
Thanks be to God.

May the almighty and merciful God; Father, Son and Holy Spirit, bless,
preserve, and keep us, this night and forevermore.

Amen.

APPENDIX B

MEDITATION TOPICS

Revised Common Lectionary: New Revised Standard Version, Three Year Cycle. Wichita, KS: St. Mark's Press, 1995.
One of the simplest and most effective ways to find a passage upon which to meditate is to use one of the lectionary readings for the coming Sunday. The stories in the Old and New Testaments are especially good for imaginative meditations, but even the Psalms can work if a phrase or idea is extracted for pondering.

Aland, Kurt, editor. *Synopsis of the Four Gospels, English Edition.* Washington, DC: United Bible Societies, 1982.
This work provides, in four columns on each page, the matching texts from the four Gospels—Matthew, Mark, Luke, and John. Comparing the different tellings of a Bible story helps me decide which version or versions to use as the meditation for a meeting.

De Mello, Anthony. *Sadhana, a Way to God: Christian Exercises in Eastern Form.* Liguori, MO: Liguori/Triumph, 1998.
De Mello explains a way into contemplation, giving forty-seven detailed, individual exercises in meditation, including the "statue meditation" used by Pamela to great effect in our groups. (See "The Famous Statue Meditation" chapter.)

Holmes, Urban Y., III. *Spirituality for Ministry.* San Francisco, CA: Harper and Row, 1982.

Pamela remembered this book being especially useful and shared with us specifically the chapters titled "The Spiritual Person," "Poverty and Plenty," and "Sexuality and Holiness."

Lindbergh, Anne Morrow. *Gift from the Sea*. New York, NY: Pantheon, 1955.
I made use of Lindbergh's image of a gift washing up on the shore along with Psalm 37:4—"Take delight in the Lord, and he will give you the desires of your heart." In meditation, we envisioned our heart's desire washing up in a bottle at our feet as we walked along the seashore. I encouraged each woman to look at her heart's desire, pick it up, examine it, ask God about it, and so on.

Linn, Dennis, Matthew, and Sheila Fabricant. *Good Goats: Healing Our Image of God*. New York, NY: Paulist Press, 1994.
———. *Sleeping with Bread: Holding What Gives You Life*. New York, NY: Paulist Press, 1995.
———. *Understanding Difficult Scripture in a Healing Way*. New York, NY: Paulist Press, 2000.
I used *Good Goats* to endeavor to heal our images of God from wrathful and judgmental to caring, saving, loving, and mothering. The second book introduced our group to a simple set of questions we could ask ourselves to discern over time God's directions for our lives. I employed the third book to encourage the group to find a loving interpretation for difficult passages of scripture, or to set such passages aside until a message of love could be found there. All three books might appear at first glance to be children's texts because of the childlike illustrations, but they are full of deep insight and wisdom.

Michael, Chester P., and Maire Norrisey. *Prayer and Temperament: Different Prayer Forms for Different Personality Types*. Charlottesville, VA: The Open Door Inc., 1991.
For the shorter weekly gatherings, I have used this text's self-graded temperament test to help find each person's temperament in the Myers-Briggs Personality Type model. Over the course of six to eight meetings, I used meditations from this book based on each of the four

temperaments. For longer "Quiet Mornings" or "Quiet Afternoons," I use this book's descriptions of the four temperaments to suggest four ways to spend the quiet time.

Metz, Barbara, S.N.D. de N., and John Burchill, O.P. *The Enneagram and Prayer: Discovering Our True Selves Befoe God.* Denville, NJ: Dimension Books, Inc., 1987.

Thomson, Clarence. *Parables and the Enneagram.* New York, NY: The Crossroad Publishing Co., 1997.

Rohr, Richard, and Andreas Ebert. *Discovering the Enneagram: An Ancient Tool for a New Spiritual Journey.* New York, NY: Crossroad, 1996.

Riso, Don Richard. *Discovering Your Personality Type.* Boston, MA, and New York, NY: Houghton Mifflin Co, 1995.

I based a nine-week series of meetings on the nine personality types of the Enneagram, using biblical characters or parables to illustrate both the redeemed and unredeemed characteristics of each type. I used the questionnaire from the Riso book to help the women find their personality type. I employed the Rohr text to help find biblical characters who illustrate the nine types. In the Metz and Burchill book, I used Appendix 5, which lists for each type "sinfulness to pray through, and giftedness to rejoice in and to pray through." I then invited the participants to meditate on any of those healthy or unhealthy traits they might find in themselves, trying to find God's invitation to see life outside their own "personality trance."

I have also given a five-part PowerPoint lecture of the nine types, using biblical characters to illustrate the redeemed and unredeemed characteristics of each type.

Metzger, Dr. Bruce M., editorial consultant. *NRSV Exhaustive Concordance.* Nashville, TN: Thomas Nelson Publishers, 1991.

This is my go-to book for finding a Bible passage I know by heart but don't know its chapter and verse. I think of the least common word in the passage and look up that word in the concordance. It works!

Nelson, Gertrude Mueller. *To Dance with God: Family Ritual and Community Celebration*. New York, NY: Paulist Press, 1986.

Bea, Holly. *Where Does God Live?* Tiburon, CA: Starseed Press, 1997.
Our group looked at the workings of the Holy Spirit at Pentecost and in our own lives, trying to name our own gifts of the Spirit. We tried to answer the questions in the children's book, *Where Does God Live?*, putting into words our personal theology, formed by the Spirit within us.

Nouwen, Henri. *Life of the Beloved: Spiritual Living in a Secular World*. New York, NY: Crossroad, 1992.
Pamela used chapters of this book over four meetings to explore how each of us was "Taken, blessed, broken, and given" as Jesus did to the bread at the last supper.

Pennington, Basil M. *Centering Prayer: Renewing an Ancient Christian Prayer Form*. Garden City, NY: Image Books, 1982.
Pamela taught us the four steps of Lectio Divina—*lectio, meditacio, oratcio*, and *contemplacio*—using this book and the biblical stories of the field and the pearl that were bought at great risk and price in Matthew 13:44–52.

Sanford, John. *Evil, the Shadow Side of Reality*. New York, NY: Crossroad, 1981.
Pamela used ideas from this book to help us explore our own shadow side, always reassuring us that, as Jung believed and Sanford reminds us, "Ninety per-cent of the shadow side is gold."

Welch, John. *Spiritual Pilgrims: Carl Jung and Teresa of Avila*. New York, NY: Paulist Press, 1982.
In this book, which compares and contrasts Jung and Teresa of Avila, Pamela shared more completely the chapter called "Serpents, Devil, and the Shadow."

Wiederkehr, Macrina. *A Tree Full of Angels: Seeing the Holy in the Ordinary*. San Francisco, CA: Harper and Row, 1990.

Wiederkehr finds meaning in her own name in the first chapter of this book. I led a meditation on listening for God naming ourselves and our loved ones, as well as naming important times and places in our lives.

APPENDIX C

FURTHER READING

Barry, William A. SJ. *Finding God in All Things: A Companion to the Spiritual Exercises of St. Ignatius.* Notre Dame, IN: Ave Maria Press, 1991.
Barry makes Ignatius's teachings beautifully understandable in everyday life.

Cunneen, Sally. *In Search of Mary: The Woman and the Symbol.* New York, NY: Ballantine Books, 1996.
Cunneen's book is one of the best of many, many writings on Mary.

Ford-Grabowsky, Mary, editor. *Spiritual Writings on Mary, Annotated and Explained.* Woodstock, VT: Skylight Paths Publishing, 2005.
Here are collected absolutely gorgeous writings about Mary, writings that kept me going during a particularly dark period of my life.

Geitz, Elizabeth Rankin, Majorie A. Burk, and Ann Smith, editors. *Women's Uncommon Prayers: Our Lives Revealed, Nurtured, Celebrated.* Harrisburg, PA: Morehouse Publishing, 2000.
I sometimes add a prayer from this wonderful volume to the closing prayer service at the end of a meeting. The title of this work is a deliberate reference to the official prayer book of the Episcopal Church, *The Book of Common Prayer.* Each prayer contributor is named, and the prayers are arranged by topic. However, I often take "a lucky dip" into this volume when searching for a prayer, and I let the book fall open where it will—to surprisingly synchronistic results!

Guenther, Margaret. *Holy Listening: The Art of Spiritual Direction.* Boston, MA: Cowley Publications, 1992.

———. *Toward Holy Ground: Spiritual Directions for the Second Half of Life.* Boston, MA: Cowley Publications, 1995.

The first volume propelled me into studying spiritual direction at General Theological Seminary, where Margaret headed the Center for Christian Spirituality. The second book cemented my desire to become a spiritual director.

Hammer, Jill. *Sisters at Sinai: New Tales of Biblical Women.* Philadelphia, PA: The Jewish Publication Society, 2001.

Jill Hammer practices midrash—retelling Biblical stories—to bring out fascinating feminist meanings in these tales of women in the Bible.

Johnson, Elizabeth A. *She Who Is: The Mystery of God in Feminist Theological Discourse.* New York, NY: The Crossroad Publishing Company, 1997.

Johnson takes a thorough look at the female aspects of the Christian/ Jewish God. I found my own way into this book by looking up each biblical passage listed in chapter 5 and delving deeper into each female God image. I crafted a four-part PowerPoint lecture on female images of God in the Bible, using images and focusing one lecture each on: God the Father, God the Son, God the Holy Spirit, and the Shekinah.

Jung, C.G. *The Red Book: Liber Novus, A Reader's Edition.* Edited and with an introduction by Sonu Shamdasani. New York, NY: W.W. Norton & Co., 2009.

Shamdasani's introduction to this book makes Jung's concepts, especially the collective unconscious and active imagination, understandable and fascinating.

Lamott, Anne. *Traveling Mercies: Some Thoughts on Faith.* New York, NY: Anchor Books, 1999.

———. *Plan B: Further Thoughts on Faith.* New York, NY: Riverhead Books, 2005.

————. *Help Thanks Wow: The Three Essential Prayers,* New York, NY: Riverhead Books, 2012.

————. *Stitches: A Handbook on Meaning, Hope and Repair.* New York, NY: Riverhead Books, 2013.

Lamott is wonderful at describing how faith can work in both the darkest and the best of times.

The Order of St. Helena. *The Saint Helena Psalter.* New York, NY: Church Publishing Incorporated, 2004.

————. *The Saint Helena Breviary.* New York, NY: Church Publishing Incorporated, 2006.

The Psalms and Services of Worship are rewritten in these valuable volumes using language that is both inclusive and beautiful, including more female images of God and more scriptural passages showing women as active participants in salvation history. Reading passages from these books is like a breath of fresh air to my soul.

Newell, J. Philip. *Celtic Benediction: Morning and Night Prayer.* Grand Rapids, MI: William B. Erdmann Publishing Co., 2000.

Newell has crafted a morning and evening liturgy of extraordinary beauty for each day of the week, focusing each day on a specific aspect of God made manifest in us and in the natural world. The striking illustrations are taken from the Lindisfarne Gospels in the British Library.

Root, Phyllis. Illustrated by Helen Oxenbury. *Big Mama Makes the World.* London, UK, Boston, MA, Sydney, Australia: Walker Books, 2002.

This is an utterly charming children's book, useful for sparking adult conversation on the Creator as Mother.

Rupp, Joyce. *Fragments of Your Ancient Name: 365 Glimpses of the Divine for Daily Meditation.* Notre Dame, IN: Sorin Books, 2011.

Rupp has crafted a short, evocative poem and a thought for each day based on names of God from different faith traditions. She gives her source for each name. Included are such fascinating God titles as

"Encourager of the Morning," "God of My Bitter Hours," "Home of Good Choices," "Transforming Presence," "Flute Player," and "Near One." I try to read a page of this lovely book every morning.

Williamson, Marianne. *Illuminated Prayers*. New York, NY: Simon & Schuster, 1997.
Williamson's touching prayers are both intimate and all-encompassing in scope. Breathtaking watercolors by Claudia Karabaic Sargent complete this book and make it an invaluable resource for daily meditation.

Winner, Lauren F. *Wearing God: Clothing, Laughter, Fire, and Other Overlooked Ways of Meeting God*. New York, NY: HarperOne, 2015.
The author opens new and exciting ways of imaging and encountering the Divine.

Printed in the United States
By Bookmasters